W9-BRB-248

Sojourner TRUTH

LIBERATED IN CHRIST

W. TERRY WHALIN

BARBOUR
PUBLISHING

ISBN 1-59310-629-7

Cover illustration © Dick Bobnick
Cover design by Douglas Miller (mhpubarts.com)

Published by Barbour Publishing, Inc., P.O. Box 719, Uhrichsville, Ohio 44683, www.barbourbooks.com

Our mission is to publish and distribute inspirational products offering exceptional value and biblical encouragement to the masses.

 Member of the
Evangelical Christian
Publishers Association

Printed in the United States of America.
5 4 3 2 1

Sojourner
TRUTH

To Bishop Phillip H. Porter Jr. and Reverend Alfred Baldwin, men who have taught me about the modern-day journey toward reconciliation. Through their lives, they continue to follow the dreams of Sojourner Truth.

To readers who from these pages experience the words of Jesus Christ—"You are truly my disciples if you keep obeying my teachings. And you will know the truth, and the truth will set you free" (John 8:31–32 NLT).

PROLOGUE

The sun was bright that cloudless day in 1851. Hundreds of men and women were settling into their seats in an Akron, Ohio, church. Normally the building was reserved for prayer, but during the next few days, it would serve as the meeting place for an annual convention on women's rights.

Should women have the same political and social rights as men? That question was the burning issue of the day, and people had traveled hundreds of miles to hear the discussion. As they waited for the opening session, a striking black woman entered the auditorium. Wearing a plain gray dress, wire-rimmed glasses, and an oversized sunbonnet, the woman stood over six feet tall and looked over fifty years old.

Seeing no empty seats in the back of the church, the woman walked slowly past the crowd of white people to the front. She stepped in a proud, almost defiant, manner. At the front of the church, the woman sat alone on one of the steps that led to the pulpit.

"Who is that?"

"Where did she come from?" The people craned their heads to see the figure.

"She looks like an abolitionist to me," someone surmised, familiar with former slaves such as Frederick Douglass, who traveled from town to town and spoke against the injustices of slavery.

At that moment, Frances Gage, who was to preside over the convention, stood on the platform. The crowd's speculation died down, and Gage introduced the first speaker. Throughout the morning, the audience heard a variety of speakers. Some were in favor of the women's rights movement, and others were against it.

The black woman with the sunbonnet sat on the pulpit steps with her face sunk into her hands. Even though she seemed distracted, she listened to every word.

At about midday, Gage called for an intermission. During the break, the black woman stood and walked among the audience. She offered to sell them copies of her book, *The Narrative of Sojourner Truth*. The book had been dictated to a friend because Sojourner couldn't read or write. It told how she had been freed from slavery and had committed her life to helping other slaves gain freedom. While working for the freedom of slaves, Sojourner Truth had realized that women also needed liberation and that her cause could be broadened to include them. During the late 1840s, Sojourner joined the fight. At first, the abolitionist and women's rights movements joined forces. Then people known as Separatists wanted to split the two movements.

When some of these separatists in Akron learned that Sojourner Truth was attending the women's rights convention, they determined that Sojourner should not speak. Several separatists gathered around Frances Gage during the lunch break and asked her to prevent Sojourner from speaking. "It will ruin our convention in the newspapers," one of them said. "Those reporters will say we are a bunch of agitators."

Gage carefully listened to each person but made no promises. "When the time comes, we'll see," she said. As it turned out, Gage didn't have to make a decision about Sojourner Truth speaking that afternoon because the former slave returned to her place on the pulpit steps and silently continued listening to the speakers. The next morning, she again appeared content to listen to the speakers, several of whom were ministers.

The first minister told the convention that men deserved greater rights and privileges because they were more intelligent than women. When the next minister spoke, he told the audience, "Men should rule over women because Jesus Christ was a man. If God wanted women to be equal with men, then He would have given some sign of His will through the birth, life, and death of the Savior."

Another preacher told the convention that women had a lower status because Eve, the first woman, had committed the original sin in the Garden of Eden. Finally a minister described how women were born inferior to men because they needed to have a man hold the door open for them. "Women don't deserve the same rights as men," the minister proclaimed, "because they are so much weaker." All of these speakers believed the Bible supported their claims that men were better than women.

A mixture of men and women were in the audience, and many of the women were visibly upset as minister after minister spoke against the rights of women. Although upset, none of these women were prepared to argue in public with such well-respected clergymen.

Then Sojourner Truth stood and walked to the pulpit. "Don't let her speak!" several men cried who sat near Frances Gage. Sojourner removed her sunbonnet and turned toward the moderator for permission to address the audience. For a brief moment, Frances Gage hesitated. Then she introduced the black woman to the audience.

Sojourner was determined to speak against these ministers. Even though she couldn't read or write, she had memorized a great deal of the Bible. She was certain that the Bible did not say women were less than men—any more than the Bible said that blacks should be slaves. She began to speak in a low, soft voice.

"Well, children, where there is so much racket, there must be something out of kilter." That "something," she said, was the domination of blacks and women by white men. "It will be fixed pretty soon," she promised the crowd.

First, Sojourner addressed the concerns of the minister who had declared women too weak to have equal rights. She explained how no one had helped her into a carriage or carried her across a mud puddle. In her entire life, no one had ever given her the best place to sit. As she spoke, Sojourner straightened her back. Her tall frame gave her words greater impact. To some people, her voice sounded like rolling thunder.

"And ain't I a woman? Look at me!" she proclaimed. "Look at my arm." Then she rolled up the sleeve on her dress. Unlike the plump arms of many women in the audience, Sojourner's arm was lean from years of hard labor.

"I have plowed and planted and gathered into barns, and no man could have done as much," she declared. "And ain't I a woman?"

She went on to describe the many times she had gone hungry, and she told about bearing children, only to watch them be sold into slavery. When she missed those children, only Jesus had been there to dry her tears.

Sojourner turned to the minister who had argued that women were less intelligent than men and therefore didn't deserve equal treatment. "What does intelligence have to do with rights?" she asked with a pointed finger and an angry stare.

Next, she addressed the minister who had argued that men should be superior because Jesus Christ was a man. "Where did your Christ come from?" she asked. The minister didn't answer. Sojourner repeated the question and answered, "From God and a woman. Man had nothing to

11

do with the birth of Jesus Christ."

Finally, she confronted the minister who had discussed Eve and the origin of sin. In defense of women, Sojourner said, "If the first woman God ever made was strong enough to turn the world upside down, all alone, these together—" she motioned toward the women in the audience—"ought to be able to turn it back and get it right side up again." Most of the audience broke out in applause. As the noise died down, she concluded, "Now old Sojourner hasn't got nothing more to say."

Many people in the audience left their seats to congratulate the black woman. She thanked them for their kind words and encouragement. For years, Sojourner Truth had traveled the country speaking on issues of freedom. And from the beginning, it had often been a long and lonely road.

ONE

Colonel Johannes Hardenbergh made the customary visit to the slave quarters on his farm near the Hudson River in upstate New York. Whenever there was a new birth on his plantation—a calf, a lamb, or a slave—the colonel inspected the new property that increased his wealth. In this case, a daughter had been born to his slaves, James and Betsey. They had named her Isabella, a name Colonel Hardenbergh liked, but in private, James and Betsey called her Belle.

"She has strong arms," the owner told the parents in Low Dutch. "She'll make a good worker." Colonel Hardenbergh spoke English when he conducted business with his neighbors, but at home he preferred to speak the language of his Dutch ancestors. Slaves had been bought and sold on farms throughout this area of New York for more than 150 years.

In 1626, Dutch settlers had come to the United States and gathered in a colony they called New Netherland. They began importing slaves from Africa to work their farms. Thirty-eight years later, the British seized the colony, changed the name to New York, and continued to bring slaves into the area. By 1723, blacks composed about 15 percent of New York's population—making them a critical part of the local economy.

The Hardenbergh estate was in a hilly neighborhood called by the Dutch name *Swartekill* (now just north of Rifton), part of the town of Hurley. It was within sight of the Catskill Mountains and near two small rivers, the Swartekill and the Wallkill, which spilled into the larger Rondout Creek about six miles before it flowed into the Hudson River.

Johannes Hardenbergh, the owner of the infant Isabella, had been a member of the New York Colonial Assembly and a colonel in the Revolutionary War. He operated a gristmill and was a large landowner. His land reached from Swartekill south for several miles along the Wallkill River. Although most of Ulster County did not have slaves, the Hardenberghs were wealthier than most families and owned seven slaves.

Although Dutch descendants like Colonel Hardenbergh learned English, they clung to their native language. They taught their slaves only Dutch so that they could better control the slaves' behavior. If the slaves couldn't speak English, they couldn't communicate with the majority of the people around them.

Belle's parents had served Hardenbergh faithfully for many years, and Belle was their eleventh child. Belle's father was a tall, strong man who was proud of his ability to do hard work. James was called Baumfree, a Low Dutch word that meant "tree." But years of hard work had taken a toll on this big man.

Betsey, Belle's mother, was a big, stocky woman with large hands. She was called Mau Mau Brett. Mau Mau Brett was much younger than Baumfree, but they loved each other and had a good marriage. Each of their other children had died or been sold into slavery. Belle's parents worried that she might be sold, as well.

Probably all of Belle's ancestors were African. Later in her life, she heard a rumor that a Mohawk Indian was among her ancestors. This rumor may have emerged to explain how straight she stood and how tall—nearly six feet. Perhaps some white people felt a need to explain Belle's intelligence by attributing it to Mohawk ancestry. No evidence supported the rumor, however, and Belle herself said, "I'm the pure African. You can see that plain enough."

The exact date of her birth is unknown because slave births weren't recorded. Some people claimed she was either born in 1776 or 1777, but it is more likely that she was born about 1797.

Slavery cast a long shadow over the lives of slave parents and their children. They had no control over their families. Often, children were taken and sold from their families. Their parents couldn't protect them. The best that Baumfree and Mau Mau Brett could do for Belle was to teach her how to handle her life.

If a slave disobeyed, punishment was often harsh, so at an early age, Belle was taught obedience. Her parents also instilled in Belle the importance of hard work, honesty, and loyalty. Another value they taught was suffering in silence. "Never make a fuss in front of the white folk," her mother told Belle. "When you've got to cry, cry alone."

When Belle was about three years old, Colonel Hardenbergh died. His son Charles had recently built a large limestone house in the nearby hills. He moved his inheritance of livestock and ten slaves, including Belle and her parents, to his new home. The new property had no slave housing, so Charles moved his slaves into the damp cellar of the stone house to eat and sleep together.

During the day, only a small amount of light came in through the tiny cellar window. At night, the slaves lit a fire in the room and slept on hard wooden pallets. If it rained, water seeped through cracks in the walls and turned the floor into a pool of mud. During the winter, the slaves huddled together around a fire to escape the bitter cold and wrapped worn-out blankets around themselves as they tried to sleep on their pallets. In the summer, the cellar was hot, humid, and smelly; so most of the time, the slaves slept outside.

In spite of the harsh living conditions, Belle's parents remained obedient to their new master and worked hard at plowing and harvesting the crops in his fields.

Consequently, their master developed some affection for the couple and eventually gave them their own land. Then Baumfree and Mau Mau Brett could raise their own corn, tobacco, and other crops to trade with their neighbors for additional food and clothing.

Soon after Belle and her parents moved to the Hardenbergh farm, her brother Peter was born. Now there was someone else for the little girl to love. One night when both children were still very young, their mother took them outside and told them to sit under a tree.

"My children," she said to them, "there is a God who hears and sees you." The two small children looked around them, but they couldn't see God.

"Where does God live?" Belle asked her mother.

"He lives in the sky," their mother answered, "and when you are beaten or cruelly treated or fall into any trouble, you must ask His help, and He will always hear and help you."

Clinging to the promise of a powerful guardian in the sky, Belle faced the difficulties in her life with increased confidence. This confidence continued to grow as Belle grew older and learned new things. On Sundays, Belle and the other slaves didn't have to work in their master's orchards or fields. Belle learned how to row a boat and ride a horse. Her mother taught her to obey her master, to recite the Lord's Prayer every day, and never to steal or lie.

One night, Belle heard her mother crying. "What's wrong, Mau Mau?" she gently asked.

"I'm groaning to think of my poor children," Mau Mau said. "They don't know where I be, and I don't know where they be. They look up at the stars, and I look up at the stars, but I can't tell where they be."

Later her mother told Belle how—many years earlier —Michael and Nancy, Belle's older brother and sister, had been snatched from their family. One snowy winter morning, some men in a horse-drawn sled stopped at the cabin where Belle's family lived. Michael was delighted when the men told him that he was going for a ride on the sled. Quickly the boy jumped onto the sled. Suddenly his joy turned to fear. One of the men walked out of the cabin with a large box containing his sister, Nancy. She was screaming.

Afraid of these men, Michael jumped off the sled, ran inside the cabin, and hid under a bed. The men came into the cabin, dragged Michael outside, put him on the sled, and then drove away. Their master had sold these children. Belle's parents never saw Michael or Nancy again.

Despite her mother's fears that Belle would be snatched away and sold to someone else, the family remained together until she was about eleven years old. In 1808, Charles Hardenbergh suddenly died, and his heirs decided to auction off his horses, cattle, and slaves.

The day of the auction, the Stone Ridge Farm was crowded with people. Belle stood trembling beside her mother. "I don't want to leave you, Mau Mau! What if they beat me? Why can't I go free like you and Baumfree?"

"Hush, Belle," her mother said softly in Dutch.

Then Belle's father, Baumfree said, "Nobody would buy a broken-down old horse like me. The law says Old Master's kin have to take care of me, so they're letting me and Mau Mau go free to get rid of us."

Almost thirty years earlier, a New York law had been passed that allowed any slave over fifty years old to be freed. The law also required that the freed slave be able to earn a living. Years of living in the cold, damp cellar had crippled Baumfree's legs and hands with arthritis. He was unable to work.

Even so, Hardenbergh's heirs decided to free both Baumfree and Mau Mau. Younger and in better health, Mau Mau could support both of them. The couple was allowed to continue living in the dark cellar as long as Mau Mau continued to work for the family. Baumfree and Mau Mau had no choice but to accept the offer and stay in the cellar. They couldn't speak any English, so they could not function in the English-speaking world around them. The couple knew Belle and Peter were headed to the slave auction.

With tears in her eyes, Mau Mau told Belle, "Child, you can't stay with us. All our other children were sold. Now it's your turn and your little brother's."

"Just remember what we've taught you, Belle," Baumfree said. "Obey your master and work hard."

Mau Mau chimed in, "And if you pray to God, He'll see that you're treated right."

A white man motioned for Belle. It was time for

her to be auctioned. "Good-bye, Mau Mau. Good-bye, Baumfree."

Belle and her brother Peter stood in the auction area. Peter was sold first to a man who didn't live in the area. Although Belle felt like crying, she stood in stony silence. Over and over, she repeated the Lord's Prayer to herself.

The auctioneer called out, "Hardenbergh's Belle, age eleven, good strong body." The girl couldn't understand the words since they were in English, but she knew it meant that she was being sold. At first no one in the crowd offered a bid. Belle thought maybe she would be allowed to stay on the farm with her parents. Then the auctioneer ordered Belle to turn to the right. When the girl did not move, the man grabbed her and turned her. "Look how tall she is, even now. She'll be a big woman in maturity, have lots of children, and be able to do a lot of work."

Still no one offered to buy Belle. She continued to pray that she would not be sold. Then the auctioneer threw in a flock of sheep, saying, "They go with the girl."

John Neely, a shopkeeper from Kingston Landing, New York, stood in the audience and recognized a bargain that he couldn't pass up. He offered one hundred dollars, and with a crack from the auctioneer's gavel, the sheep and Belle were sold. Belle had a new master.

While Neely thought he had struck a good deal, his wife was not impressed. "This girl can't speak English," she yelled at her husband. "Sure, she looks strong, but what good is she for me? When I ask for a pot, she gives me a spoon. When I ask for a skillet, she hands me a broom." When Belle couldn't understand Mrs. Neely's instructions and responded in Dutch, Mrs. Neely beat Belle. Belle tried to learn English from her new masters, but Mrs. Neely had no patience for teaching. War was declared between Mrs. Neely and her young slave, and Belle had no chance of winning. Mrs. Neely repeatedly slapped Belle. "I told you the word for that thing is broom! Broom! Say broom!"

One day Mrs. Neely's frustrations grew unbearable. That Sunday morning, she sent her slave out to the barn where Mr. Neely was waiting for her. In the barn, Belle found her master heating some metal rods over red-hot coals. Without offering any explanation, Mr. Neely grabbed Belle's hands and tied them together. He tore Belle's shirt off her back and began to beat the girl's back with the rods. Belle pleaded with her master to stop and called out to God for help. Finally she fainted. Belle lay in the straw, soaked with her own blood, and wept bitterly. It was her first beating, and she determined to do whatever was necessary to avoid another one.

Afterward, Belle crept off into the woods and cried out to God. "Was it right for them to beat me, God? You've got to get me a new master. You have to help me, God." But Belle's prayers were not instantly answered.

Mrs. Neely continued to scream at her young slave with confusing instructions, but Belle learned how to cope. On her own initiative, Belle scrubbed the floors so clean that Mrs. Neely had no cause to complain. Slowly,

Belle learned to speak some English, but her first language, Dutch, always showed in her accented speech.

As Belle worked for the Neelys, she sometimes wondered, *Will I ever see my family again?* One winter evening, when Belle had almost lost hope of seeing her family, her father arrived at the Neely home. Baumfree looked old and very sick. He told Belle how a family named Simmons had rented the Big House but permitted her parents to continue living in the cellar. Mau Mau worked hard, but they barely had enough money to buy food or clothing.

Belle listened to her father and didn't mention her own struggles. Baumfree noticed that despite the deep snow on the ground, his daughter didn't have warm clothing or shoes. When he asked about it, Belle explained, "I can't wear Mrs. Neely's hand-me-downs. They are too small."

As her father prepared to leave, he hugged Belle, but she drew back in pain. Baumfree walked out to the gate of the property. Belle followed her father through the snow by stepping in his large footprints. Once the pair was out of the Neelys' sight, Belle showed him her scarred back. Baumfree was filled with rage at her beating, but even worse was the knowledge that he hadn't been able to protect his daughter. Although Baumfree was old and crippled, he was free. He vowed to use his freedom to help his daughter.

As he left, Baumfree promised Belle that he would try to help her. Unfortunately for Belle, change took time. She continued working for the Neely family.

After about two years with the Neelys, God answered what Belle later called a "desperate prayer." Somehow old Baumfree persuaded Martin Schryver to purchase Belle from the Neelys for $105. The fisherman didn't own any other slaves but had a farm and a tavern on the Rondout Creek. This new location was only about five miles from the Neely farm.

Belle worked hard for her new owner, partially from gratitude but partially from fear of receiving another beating. The Schryvers were a coarse and uneducated couple, but they weren't cruel. They spoke both English and Dutch, so Belle could easily talk with them. Without someone yelling at her constantly, Belle's English became much more fluent.

The Schryvers treated Belle well, although sometimes she felt uncomfortable around the coarse men who frequented their tavern. A hard worker, Belle hoed corn-fields, hauled in fish, and gathered roots and herbs for the homemade beer sold in the tavern. She had a great deal of freedom to roam outdoors. Occasionally watching the many white-sailed sloops on the Hudson River, she was startled to see one of the new steamboats throwing up black smoke.

Once when Belle was about thirteen, a "grand ball" was held at Schryvers' tavern. She was fascinated to watch the women wearing high-crowned white caps and starched and ironed dresses. As dancers pranced around the tavern, they shouted out a popular song, "Washington's Ball," which celebrated George Washington for planting the tree of liberty. After hearing this song at the ball, Belle was able to sing it for the rest of her life.

With her new owners, Belle had plenty to eat. She grew almost six feet tall before she turned fourteen years old. During the winter, Belle had a warm shawl and even shoes—a cast-off pair from her master because women's shoes were too small for her large feet.

Unfortunately, Belle's parents were doing poorly as freed slaves. They found it difficult to get enough food to eat and grew ill. Too soon, Mau Mau Brett grew sick and died. Mr. Simmons came to the Schryvers to take Belle to the funeral. He explained to Belle, "This past winter was very hard. One day Baumfree had gone out to do a small chore for pennies. When he returned to the cellar, he found Mau Mau in a coma. By morning, she'd died."

Belle and her brother Peter were both able to attend their mother's funeral and visit their father. Poor Baumfree was grief-stricken. He cried out, "Oh, I had thought God would take me out first—Mau Mau was so much smarter than me and could get about and take care of herself, and I am so old and helpless. What will happen to me? I can't do anything anymore; my children are all gone, and here I am left helpless and alone."

Despite her concern for her father, Belle couldn't do anything for Baumfree. She had to return to the Schryver family. She prayed that God would give her a means to help her father.

While working at the tavern, Belle overheard many conversations about slavery. Her ears perked up whenever the people began talking about abolition. It was a new English word that Belle had learned. The abolitionists were people who wanted to end slavery. While Belle did not understand much about it, she knew that if she were free, she'd go straight to Baumfree.

"Whoever these abolitionists are, God," Belle prayed, "please bless their work."

Soon afterward, Belle received a message that her father, Baumfree, had starved to death. After Mau Mau's death, Baumfree had been allowed to continue living on the Hardenbergh estate along with two other slaves. But soon the other slaves died, and Baumfree was left in the cellar alone. Too sick to care for himself, Baumfree lived his last few months cold, filthy, and forgotten.

When the Hardenbergh family learned of the old man's death, they donated a pine box and a jug of whiskey for mourners. It was their final tribute to a man who had been a faithful, kind, and honest servant.

Other than Peter, Belle had no known immediate family still living. She felt alone, and God seemed so distant. In her own determined way, Belle decided to pray for the only thing left: her freedom. She remembered the words of Mau Mau about the great God in the sky: "God is always with you. You are never alone."

Perhaps the rumors that I heard were true. Maybe the slaves in New York will be freed after all, Belle thought.

TWO

One day, a short, ruddy-faced man came into the tavern. As Belle served the various customers, this man began a conversation with Schryver.

"That slave girl yours?" the man inquired.

"Yes, Belle is thirteen, and she'll grow to be well over six feet," Schryver said.

"I need this girl to help out on my farm in New Paltz," the man said. "I'll buy her for three hundred dollars."

The price was three times what the Schryvers had paid. Although the couple didn't approve of slavery and had plans to free Belle when she reached eighteen, three hundred dollars was a lot of money in those days. The Schryvers accepted the offer, and Belle had a new master, John Dumont.

The farmer was pleased with his purchase and recorded in a book dated 1810 that Belle was "about thirteen," but "stands nearly six feet tall." When Belle came to the Dumonts' farm, the ten other slaves welcomed her and gave the new slave a quick description of her new master.

On most accounts, according to the slaves, Mr. Dumont was a decent man and didn't deal out excessive punishment. They said, "He doesn't believe in separating families, and if you do your work and don't make trouble, then you'll get along fine."

When the slaves began to talk about the mistress of the house, they told a completely different story. "Watch your step around Mrs. Dumont," they said. "She's got a spiteful tongue and a sour temperament. As much as possible, keep away from her because it will only get you into trouble."

Keeping away from Mrs. Dumont was impossible for Belle since she worked part-time in the Big House, and Mrs. Dumont took an instant dislike to her quiet-spoken new slave. Mrs. Dumont pulled the two white maids aside and told them, "Isabella should be taught a lesson. Make sure you grind down her proud attitude."

Despite the harsh treatment from her mistress and coworkers in the Dumont house, Belle remembered her mother's lessons on obedience, so she always tried hard to please her owners. Sometimes the other slaves chided Belle saying, "Girl, you're too obedient for Master and Miss Dumont."

Throughout her childhood, Belle had been taught to repay evil with good. She had developed a deep belief that her hard work would eventually be rewarded.

One of Belle's many duties was to wash and boil the potatoes first thing in the morning. Mysteriously, each time Mrs. Dumont reached the kitchen, the potatoes were boiling in dirty water. "You didn't wash these potatoes," Mrs. Dumont scolded Belle. The girl knew she was innocent and tried to explain. The denial only made Mrs. Dumont more angry. Belle stopped protesting and looked for another way to prove her innocence.

The next morning, Belle scrubbed the potatoes even harder and longer to make sure all of the dirt was removed. Yet when Mrs. Dumont inspected the pot, the potatoes were once again cooking in dirty water.

The Dumonts' ten-year-old daughter Gertrude liked Belle. Later that night, Gertrude called Belle into her room. She told Belle, "I suspect that Kate is at the bottom of this mysterious dirt in the potatoes." Kate was another maid who obviously disliked Belle.

Gertrude created a plan to catch Kate in the act. Belle listened with surprise and amazement. It marked the first time a white person had offered to help her out of trouble.

The next day, Belle once again washed the potatoes and put them into the pot to boil. True to her plan, Gertrude hid in the kitchen and waited. As usual, Belle went outside to milk the cows in the barn.

Immediately after Belle left the kitchen, Kate came into the kitchen and dumped a clump of ashes into the pot. Gertrude jumped out from her hiding place and said,

"I caught you, Kate!" She hurried off to tell her parents, and with the help of Gertrude, Belle's name was cleared.

Belle was growing into a teenager, and while she had the body of a woman, she had the mind of a young girl. Since there weren't any adults Belle felt she could confide in, she made her own decisions and solved her own problems. Sometimes these decisions were incorrect or based on faulty beliefs.

Belle decided that Master Dumont was a god. She reasoned that God knew everything, so He must know about slavery. And if the Lord of the Universe knew about slavery and didn't—or couldn't—stop it, then her master had to be very powerful—almost a god himself.

Convinced that her master was an all-seeing and all-knowing god, Belle was driven by fear. To gain favor with Dumont, Belle often worked until she dropped from exhaustion. Convinced that her master could know her thoughts, Belle told him everything—even reporting the actions of her fellow slaves.

Dumont often bragged about the hardworking Belle. "Why, she could do a good family's washing in the night and be ready in the morning to go to the field. Then Belle could still do as much raking and binding as my best hands," he told his neighbors.

When the master talked about Belle in this manner, the other slaves grew impatient and critical of her. They called her, "white folks' nigger," and drove her out of their circle of friends. The other slaves couldn't understand Belle's confusion and hurt.

One day, Cato, the Dumonts' driver, took Belle aside and said, "What's the matter with you, gal? Can't you see you only hurtin' the rest of us when you work yourself to death like you doin'? Next thing we know, the master'll be expectin' us all to work like that. Where'll we find the time to take care of our own children then? When is old people gonna rest? Workin' hard ain't gonna free any of us. Just kill us sooner, that's all."

From Cato, who also served as the slaves' preacher, Belle learned that God didn't always answer prayers immediately or stop evil people in their tracks. Cato told Belle, "He studies on the situation, hoping the evildoers will make a change of heart and correct themselves." Through her talk with Cato, Belle began to understand the human side of her master. Dumont wasn't a god, and if he wasn't a god, then Belle didn't need to be afraid all the time. She could talk to the great God in the sky without her master hearing her pleas for help and understanding. For a while, this conversation with Cato lifted the heavy burden of confusion from Belle's heart.

When Belle's attitude toward Dumont changed, the other slaves began to trust her again. But she still felt lonely without any family around. Through her years with Dumont, Belle came to accept that loneliness would be her companion—until one day she met a special friend named Robert.

Fifty days after Easter, the slaves got a break from their grueling work on the farm. The holiday was called

Pinxter, the Dutch word for Pentecost, and for a full week the slaves were given time off from work. If they chose to work, they were paid for it. At Pinxter, slave and master enjoyed good food, good company, and fun.

Belle and the rest of the Dumonts' slaves went to a clearing where the slaves' chosen leader waited for them under a large oak tree. Prince Gerald, as he was called because some people said he was the son of a British soldier and an African princess from the Congo, stood well over seven feet tall—an imposing height. Well known for his athletic skill, he challenged the men to contests of strength and endurance. Most of the young men dreamed of dethroning Prince Gerald, but for as long as Belle could remember, no one had managed to beat the prince.

After the contests, the feasting started and was followed by endless dancing to the beat of drums. Couples clapped and sang far into the night. At dawn the weary slaves rested, but at sunset the activities began again.

During this Pinxter celebration, Belle allowed herself to be happy. Robert, a handsome young slave from a nearby estate, came up to Belle and introduced himself. Perhaps the joy of the festivities created her feelings, but for Belle, it was love at first sight.

The young couple shared a lunch of summer sausage, gingerbread, and cider. Then they talked and enjoyed the dancing. After Pinxter, they continued to meet whenever they could break away from work. Slaves were not citizens and could not be legally married, although many couples were allowed to live together as man and wife.

Robert's owner, a man named Catlin, was opposed to the relationship between Robert and Belle. Catlin was only interested in building up his estate. He wanted his female slaves to have lots of children whom Catlin could either sell or put to work in his fields. He ordered Robert to stop meeting with Belle and to take a wife from one of the female slaves on his estate.

Despite his owner's command, Robert insisted on continuing to sneak off and see Belle. Catlin became suspicious that the relationship was continuing, so he set a trap for the disobedient slave.

One afternoon a slave told Robert, "Belle is sick and needs your help." Immediately, Robert stopped working and ran off to see Belle. In actuality, Belle was in good health and working in the Dumont kitchen. Catlin and his son were waiting to spring the trap outside the Dumont home.

Belle heard loud screams right outside her kitchen window. She looked out in horror as Catlin and his son beat Robert with heavy sticks. Master Dumont also heard the commotion and came running. Belle pleaded with her master to help Robert.

Dumont broke the gentleman's agreement between slaveholders and stopped Catlin from reprimanding his slave. "I won't tolerate that kind of beating on this farm," he yelled angrily. "You won't kill him here!" Dumont recognized that Robert was receiving an unusually severe beating. Most beatings were to keep slaves from disobeying, but the Catlins looked like they wanted to kill Robert.

When the beating stopped, the Catlins yanked Robert to his feet, bound his hands, and marched him away. Dumont followed the Catlins home to make sure that Robert wasn't actually killed. But the Catlins were satisfied: The beating had changed Robert's attitude. While his body continued to live, his spirit was completely broken.

As Belle watched Robert be beaten and hauled off in chains, she felt each lash in her heart. The only way she could cope with such a painful experience was to shut down her emotions. For a few minutes, Belle slipped away from the Dumont house to a secluded spot at a creek. She sat under a clump of willow trees. There in the quietness, Belle prayed and sang the songs her African grandmother had taught Mau Mau Brett. Alone, she felt the freedom to cry, so Belle cried long and hard. Then, just as she had been taught from childhood, Belle dried her tears, put away her hurt, and returned to work. She never saw Robert again.

One day, as John Dumont stood in the distance watching his slaves, he thought, *It's time for Belle to get married and begin to have children. Tom would make a good husband for her.* Dumont had purchased Tom as a young man, and he had worked many years on the farm. To Dumont, it made no difference that Belle and Tom did not love each other. They were just two slaves.

When Belle learned of her master's decision, she insisted that a real preacher marry them. Dumont must have seen Belle's determination because he agreed to the request, and a black preacher married the couple.

Belle could see that her husband had at one time been a good-looking man, but when she married him, he was stooped and old from his years of hard labor in the fields. Before long, the young bride learned that Tom had also suffered heartache and loss. Years earlier, his love had been sold away from him to a family in New York City. Enraged and hurt by the sudden loss of his wife, Tom ran away on foot to the large city so he could find her. With the help of freed slaves in the city, Tom managed to stay away from the Dumont farm for a month. He never located his wife, but slave trackers caught Tom and returned him to the estate.

Belle reached out and gently touched the scars on her husband's back and neck. She wept from the memory of her own beatings. The wounds from their terrible whippings had scarred over, but the memories were seared into their minds forever.

In their own way, Tom and Belle loved each other. Belle was considerate and caring for her husband, and Tom was quiet and agreeable. After a year of marriage, the couple had a daughter named Diana. During the next twelve years, Belle gave birth to four more children: Elizabeth, Hannah, Peter, and Sophia. Each child learned the lessons that Belle had learned from her mother: Never steal, never lie, and always obey your master.

While taking on the duties of a mother and wife, Belle continued her hard work for the Dumonts. Her life was increasingly complicated with nursing and caring for her children. Sometimes she strapped one of her children to her back as she hoed a field. Other times, she tied an old sheet to the branch of a tree and had the older children watch the younger child in a makeshift swing. Other slaves on the Dumont farm also helped raise each other's children.

Year after year, Belle chopped wood, planted corn, and hauled buckets of water for the Dumonts, but she never gave up hope that one day she would be free. In 1824, she finally learned the good news. Pressured by abolitionist groups, the New York State legislature had passed an emancipation law. The law required that all slaves born before July 4, 1799, be freed on July 4, 1827. Male slaves born after that date were to gain their freedom when they turned twenty-eight, and female slaves were to be freed after their twenty-fifth birthday.

Belle struggled over the date of her birthday. No one was certain of the exact day, but the Dumonts agreed that Belle would be eligible for freedom in 1827. The slaves looked forward to what they called "Freedom Day." Even though three years stood between her and Freedom Day, just the idea of freedom put a bounce in Belle's step. She sang while she worked and kept her sights set unswervingly on freedom.

One day in 1825, Dumont came to Belle with an offer for her freedom. He complimented her on her hard work for the past fifteen years. Two more years remained until he was required by law to set Belle free.

"I'll let you go a year earlier than the law says I need to if you promise to work extrahard for me," Dumont said. "And as a bonus, I'll let Tom go free with you, and you can live in the cabin that I own down the road."

Belle accepted the offer. Over the next several months, she put in extralong hours of hard work—planting, washing, cooking, cleaning. Then in the spring, Belle cut her hand on the blade of a scythe. Because she didn't slow down and care for the wound, it didn't heal properly. Despite the way the wound bled and hurt, Belle never missed a day's work. The thought of freedom kept her going. When the year ended, Belle had fulfilled her promise to Dumont.

She waited for Dumont to free her, but he didn't say a word about the agreement. Finally she could stand it no longer. She burst into the house and confronted her master.

With arrogance in his voice and a wave of his hand, Dumont told Belle, "Our deal is off. Go back to work." Dumont had probably originally planned to free Belle as he had said. That year, however, the Hessian fly had killed most of his crops, and he was facing financial ruin and needed all his slaves—especially Belle—to plant the spring crops and make a new start.

If the master had approached Belle with the problem his crop failure had created, they might have worked out some agreement. But instead the master betrayed Belle's trust.

Belle was furious at the curt dismissal from her

master. "Why won't you honor your word?"

Dumont searched for any excuse. Then he noticed her bandaged hand and said, "You can't expect me to free you. With a hurt hand, you can't expect me to believe that you've put in extra work."

Belle touched her injured hand, stiff and twisted from hard work and neglect. Anger exploded like the steam roaring from a kettle on a hot stove. She saw a true picture of her master—a little man whose words were small and meaningless. Without bothering to argue or defend herself, Belle turned and walked away. In her mind, she was a free woman and had stopped being Dumonts' Belle. Those days were over!

Belle decided to run away. When she escaped, she wouldn't be able to take her children with her, and she wanted to leave on somewhat good terms with Dumont. So she decided that she would first finish spinning the annual harvest of wool. However, the Dumonts' sheep yielded more wool than usual that year. By the time Belle finished her spinning, it was late autumn.

THREE

Early one fall morning, Belle gathered together her five children, ranging in age from twelve years to less than a year. It was time for a serious talk with them and her husband. Diana, Elizabeth, Hannah, Peter, and baby Sophia listened quietly to their mother.

"Mr. Dumont has cheated me out of my freedom, and I'll not let him get away with it," Belle explained to Tom and her children. "I've got to run away and I can't take you with me, but I'll be back for you. Someday we'll be together again."

Tom objected to his wife's attitude, "Belle, calm down. It's not worth trying to escape, because we'll be free anyway in another year." But Tom couldn't dissuade his wife. Belle was determined to escape.

When is the best time to escape? Belle wondered. In some ways, night seemed the best hour to run away because of the darkness, but Belle was afraid of the dark. Escaping during the day was much too dangerous because someone would surely see her.

As she searched for an answer, Belle prayed for guidance, and the Lord showed her a solution. The best time for her to escape would be sometime between the night and the day—at dawn. There would be just enough light to calm her fears; yet in the early morning hour, the Dumonts and their neighbors would still be asleep. Fearing her plans might be discovered, Belle told no one her exact plans for escape—not even Tom and her children.

On the morning of her escape, Belle woke up before dawn, gathered together some food and clothing, and wrapped them in a large piece of cloth. Next Belle bundled up Sophia, whom she'd decided to take with her. As she slowly walked out of the cabin, Belle knew it would be difficult to leave her other children and Tom, but she knew the other slaves would take good care of them. Belle left the Dumont farm just as the sun was starting to light the sky. When full daylight arrived, she was far from her master's house.

At the top of a hill, Belle stopped to rest and scan the horizon. No one was following her, yet she was still troubled. She had no idea where to go or what to do to be safe from Dumont. Once again, she turned to God for direction.

While Belle was praying, a memory flickered into her mind. Long ago, she had been walking along the road when a stranger had stopped her. He'd said, "It's not right that you should be a slave. God does not want it." At the time, Belle had believed Master Dumont was like a god, so she'd told her master about the exchange.

"Forget that kind of talk, Belle," Dumont had ordered, and she'd promptly obeyed him. Now, as she walked along the road and prayed, Belle remembered the man, Levi Rowe, a Quaker who lived down the road from the Dumont estate. Generally, Quakers were active abolitionists—a word that Belle had never forgotten.

She decided to ask Rowe for help. In the early morning light, Belle walked to his house and knocked on his door. It took a long time for him to answer because he was old and very ill.

In quick bursts of emotion, the frightened runaway slave poured out her story, and Levi Rowe patiently listened. Rowe was too ill to help Belle, but he directed her to the home of a Quaker couple named Isaac and Maria Van Wagener. "Maybe this couple could hide you," the farmer told Belle with concern on his face.

Belle thanked Mr. Rowe for his advice and continued her journey with fresh hope. She had known the Van Wageners since her childhood. A few miles down the road, Belle reached their home. After hearing Belle's story, the couple welcomed Belle inside and offered her a job and place to stay.

A short time later, Dumont arrived at the Van Wagener home. He was searching for his slave and suspected the Quakers had offered her shelter. Confronting his longtime slave, Dumont threatened Belle with harsh punishment for running away at night.

"I did not run away at night," Belle responded calmly. "I walked away by day."

"This argument will not work for you," Dumont said. "I insist that you return at once."

Again Belle refused. Dumont tried another tactic. "I know where you are, Belle. When you are not looking, I'll steal Sophia, and then you'll come back."

"No, Mr. Dumont," Belle said with firmness. "Your threats don't frighten me. I'm not coming back!"

As the Van Wageners watched the struggle between Belle and her master, Mr. Van Wagener offered to buy Belle for twenty dollars and her baby for five dollars. Dumont could see that Belle wasn't going to return to his farm, and even if she did return, she wouldn't work hard for him as she had in the past. He accepted Van Wagener's offer and left in a huff.

"Thank you, Master Van Wagener," Belle said as she addressed her new owner.

"Belle, you and Sophia are free," the Quaker said. "There is but one Master, and He who is your Master is my Master."

Through the winter, Belle worked for the Van Wageners. The kind and gentle couple welcomed her in all ways. They lived simply, without a lot of frills. Often they sat for hours meditating on the Bible and praying— never saying a word. Such a life marked a sharp contrast to the storytelling and constant chatter in the Dumont slave quarters. On the Dumont estate, slaves never went to church or read the Bible.

Although content to stay with the Van Wageners, the thought of losing her children tempted Belle to return to the Dumont estate. Years later, Belle told friends that a powerful force turned her around whenever she tried to leave.

"Jesus stopped me," she explained simply. Her spiritual experience was so powerful that Belle never again seriously considered returning to her old master. Freedom Day, when all of the slaves would be freed, was getting closer every day.

But Freedom Day didn't arrive soon enough. One day, Belle learned that Dumont had sold her only son, Peter, to a Dr. Gedney. The new owner planned to take the boy to England with him as a body servant. To make matters worse, Mr. Van Wagener learned that Dr. Gedney had taken Peter to New York City before discovering that the boy was too young to serve him properly. So Dr. Gedney had gone on alone to England. Before leaving, he'd sent the boy to his brother, Solomon Gedney, in New Paltz. Solomon had sold Peter to a wealthy Alabama planter named Fowler, who had just married the Gedneys' sister Liza.

When Belle heard that Peter was headed to the South, she was furious. She hurried to the Dumonts and confronted her old master with anger and determination. From Belle's perspective, Dumont had started the chain of events with his initial sale.

"Alabama is a slave-for-life state," Belle said angrily to her former master. "There is no way Peter will ever be free. If you hadn't sold him, he wouldn't be there." Belle pleaded with Dumont for his help.

Mr. Dumont contended that he knew nothing about Peter's movement to Alabama. He had sold Peter to Dr. Gedney as a body servant, and that was all he knew about the situation.

Mrs. Dumont especially infuriated Belle with her reaction. "Ugh! A fine fuss to make about a little nigger! Why, haven't you got as many children left as you can take care of? It's a shame you aren't all back in Africa! Why are you making such a hullabaloo about the neighborhood, and all about a paltry nigger!"

Belle burned with anger, but she made certain her response was slow and deliberate. "I'll have my child again."

"How can you get him?" asked Mrs. Dumont. "And what have you to support him with if you could? Have you any money?"

"No," Belle replied. "I have no money, but God has enough."

Years later, Belle recalled her feelings about the exchange. "I knew I'd have Peter again and was sure that God would help me get him. Why, I felt so tall within— as if the power of the nation was with me!"

Because Belle got no aid from her former master, she turned to Solomon Gedney's mother, from whom she received even less compassion. The old woman laughed at Belle. "Is your child better than my child? My daughter

44

has gone to Alabama, and yours has gone to live with her, to have enough of everything and to be treated like a gentleman."

Belle combined sorrow, fear, and indignation in her response. "Yes, your child has gone there to Alabama, but she is married, and my boy has gone as a slave. Peter is too little to go so far from his mother." Mrs. Gedney laughed and sent the distressed mother away.

Belle walked along the road and prayed, "Show those around me that You are my helper!" She turned once again to the Quaker abolitionists for help. A number of them met at the Van Wageners' home to discuss her plight and what they could do to help.

"Peter's sale was against the law, Belle," they told her. A New York state law forbade selling slaves out of state. If Solomon Gedney was found guilty, he would face a fourteen-year jail sentence and perhaps a stiff financial penalty. Peter would immediately be freed.

The Van Wageners recommended that Belle seek help from their friends in Poppletown, a town near Kingston, New York. She would need to file suit against Solomon Gedney.

It took Belle a good part of a day to walk to Poppletown, and she felt bone tired when she finally reached the home of the Van Wageners' friends. The hostess graciously offered Belle supper and a clean bed for the night.

As Belle entered the bedroom and shut the door, she was frightened. She had never been offered such a nice, clean, beautiful white bed. It never occurred to her that she was supposed to sleep in the bed. For a while she slept underneath the bed; then she decided that if she didn't use the bed, she might insult her hostess.

The next morning, the family took Belle to the courthouse. As frightened as she had been by the prospect of sleeping in a clean white bed, Belle was even more terrified by the large stone courthouse. Determined to get back her son, she gathered her courage and walked inside. Belle managed to get directions for where to go and what to do, and then she filed a complaint against Solomon Gedney.

When the grand jury heard Belle's case, they decided in her favor. Belle's Quaker friends had helped her hire a lawyer, Esquire Chipp, and he helped Belle make out a writ. She took the legal document to the constable of New Paltz. The document ordered Solomon Gedney to appear before the court with Peter.

Unfortunately, the constable served the document on the wrong man. This gave Solomon Gedney advance warning. Gedney slipped away to Mobile, Alabama, before the constable realized his mistake with the paperwork. For months, all Belle could do was wait.

In the spring, Belle heard that Gedney had returned to New Paltz, so she went to his home to claim her son. "That boy is mine," Gedney barked, slamming the door in her face.

Belle refused to back down. She visited Attorney Chipp again. This time, the writ was properly served on the right man. Gedney appeared in court and paid a six-hundred-dollar bond, promising to appear in court and face the charges that he had sold Peter out of state.

Just when things looked promising, Belle faced another delay. Her attorney told Belle that her case would have to wait several months until court was in session. Belle complained about this new delay, but Chipp asked her to be patient with the court system.

"I cannot wait. I must have Peter now!" Belle cried.

Chipp could think of nothing else that could be done to speed up Belle's case, so he sent her away.

While walking back to the Van Wageners' home, Belle met a man on the road. He greeted her and asked, "Have they returned your son to you yet?"

Belle told the man the latest news and that she didn't know what else to do.

The man pointed to a stone house. "The lawyer Demain lives there. Go to him and tell him your case with Peter. I think he'll help you with it, but stick with the man, and don't give him a moment's peace until he helps you."

After Demain heard the details of Belle's case, he promised to return Peter within twenty-four hours for a fee of five dollars. Belle's Quaker friends gave her the money, and Demain went to the courthouse. He quickly returned with bad news. Peter didn't want to return to his mother. Reportedly, Peter had fallen to his knees and begged to stay with his master.

The next morning, everyone involved in the case appeared before the judge in his chambers.

"No, she's not my mother!" Peter explained to the judge.

"What about that scar on your forehead?" the judge asked. "How did you get that?"

"The Fowlers' horse kicked me," Peter answered.

"And what about this other scar on your cheek? How did that happen?" the judge continued.

"I accidentally ran against a carriage," Peter said. The judge wasn't fooled for a minute. One look into the boy's eyes made it clear that he was terrified of his master.

The judge awarded the boy to his mother. It was official. After Gedney left the room and Peter was re-assured that he didn't have to go with his former master, the boy cautiously changed his story. "This woman looks a little like my mother," he said.

Belle had won freedom for her son and could take Peter home. That evening, as she prepared Peter for bed, Belle noticed that his back was streaked with old and fresh wounds. "Peter," Belle whispered gently to her son, "what kind of monster would do this to a six-year-old?"

Peter finally told the truth. "Master Gedney told me to say that I didn't know you," he explained as tears ran down his cheeks. "He said that if I didn't say what he wanted, then I would get the worst whipping I've ever had."

"Now, now, child," Belle said as she held her son in her arms. "You're free now and safe with me." As she thought about the chain of events over the last several days, Belle was certain the man on the road who had pointed her to Demain was an angel from heaven. She thanked God for His answer and for freedom for Peter.

Then Belle touched the scarred back of her small son. She was angry about his beatings and treatment. She called on God to give them a double portion of what had been taken away.

As her son heard his mother, he said, "This is nothing, Mamma. You should see Phillis. She had a little baby, and Fowler cut her until the milk as well as blood ran down her body. It would scare you to see Phillis."

Belle didn't think about the fact that she was one of the first black women in the United States to win a court case. She was simply happy to have her son restored to her.

"God," she prayed, "if You will, no child of mine will be sold away from me again!"

FOUR

After Belle gained Peter's freedom, she stayed in Kingston, New York, where she found work with a family named Latin. Peter continued living with Belle, but Sophia, at about age two, went to live with her other sisters, who were still on the Dumont estate.

On July 4, 1827, Tom, Belle's husband, was freed. Belle was still in Kingston, and Tom was living in the town of New Paltz. The couple found it impossible to build a home together, and in time they grew apart. Until his health failed, Tom did odd jobs in the area, but he died before the end of the year.

While Belle lived in Kingston, she did laundry for one of Solomon Gedney's relatives. One day, as she hung out the wash on the clothesline, Belle heard a scream from inside the house. She listened as a letter was read aloud from the Alabama authorities. Liza

Fowler's husband had beaten his wife to death. The letter explained that Fowler had gone mad and would be kept locked up, "for the rest of his unhappy life."

Belle remembered the scars on her young son's back. She asked Peter, "Was there anybody who tried to help you, boy?"

Peter answered with a pained look across his face, "Oh, Mammy, sometimes I crawled underneath the stoop with blood running from my back. Sometimes Miz Liza would come and grease my sores, when everyone was in bed and asleep."

Before long, Belle and Peter left Kingston and returned to the Van Wageners. The couple welcomed them back and provided work for Belle. She clung to her dream of having all her children under one roof; but for the time being, all she could do was be near them. She settled her differences with the Dumonts, and they allowed her to visit her daughters regularly.

While living with the Van Wageners, Belle became so comfortable that she nearly forgot about God. In her way of thinking, God was someone a person called on for help in trouble. Since Belle was comfortable, why should she call on God? As time passed, she became bored by the simple life of the Van Wageners. As the big slave holiday of Pinxter approached, Belle thought about giving up her freedom and returning to the Dumont estate. Then she could sing, drink, smoke, and dance with her slave friends.

But as her 1850 narrative reports, "God revealed

Himself to me with all of the suddenness of lightning." She cried out, "Oh, God, how big You be!" Being overwhelmed with the presence of God's greatness, Belle fell on her hands and knees, trying to crawl away from the Almighty, but she could find no place to hide.

Then Belle felt the wickedness of her life and the need for someone to speak to God for her. Years later, Belle described this moment as her conversion to Christ. A space opened between her and God, and in the space she suddenly saw Jesus. She said later, "I felt Jesus come between God and me as sensibly as I ever felt an umbrella raised over my head. . . . I saw the hair on His head, and I saw His cheek, and I saw Him smile, and I have seen the same smile on people since."

After this experience, Belle preached as she worked in the kitchen. Mr. Van Wagener felt it was a nuisance to listen to her preach all day. Belle's conversion not only saved her life, but it also drastically changed how she related to other people. Later in her life, she explained, "I was civilized not by people, but by Jesus. When I got religion, I found some work to do to benefit somebody."

Before Belle found a relationship with Jesus Christ, she admitted that she had urged God to kill "all the white people and not leave enough for seed." But after her conversion, she said, "Yeah, God, I love everyone and the white people, too."

Belle remembered her time with the Van Wageners as some of the happiest months of her life. "Oh, everything at the Van Wageners was so pleasant and kind and good and all so comfortable," she said later. "Enough of everything; indeed, it was beautiful!" When the work for the day was finished, Mr. Van Wagener pulled out his Bible and read aloud to Belle and the others. These lessons from God's Word gave Belle a better understanding of the relationship between God and humanity.

During those months at the Van Wageners, Peter's body began to heal, but Belle realized he also needed emotional healing. As a child, Peter enjoyed running and playing along the wharves in New Paltz. Huge ships came into port, to Peter's great excitement. He thrilled at the sailors' stories of adventures.

Then Peter began to steal and, when caught, lie about it. At first, Belle wasn't too hard on her son because of his difficult past, but she knew that she needed to help him. She tried to keep Peter occupied by having him work for a man who managed the river locks on Rondout Creek. She thought it would fill Peter's days and keep him out of trouble. Instead Peter grew worse.

Then Belle tried to locate a church home for Peter. Maybe then Peter wouldn't stray from his mother's teachings. A new Methodist church had opened in New Paltz. One Sunday morning, Belle put on her good black dress and dressed Peter for church. Neither one of them had any shoes, but Belle decided that shoes didn't matter to God. They walked to church.

The Methodist meeting was held in a private house. Knowing that it was not customary for blacks to enter white meetings unless they sat in a separate "Negro pew,"

Belle was afraid to enter the house. So she stood outside the house and peered in through the open window.

The preacher, a circuit rider named Mr. Ferriss, read the words of a hymn, "There is a holy city, a world of light above," that described the immortal life that awaited the faithful. Line by line, he sang it and thumped the floor with its rhythm. The congregation sang after him. Outside, Belle also learned the hymn and remembered it for the rest of her life.

While Belle delighted in the music, she still wondered if she should walk inside with Peter. Then she remembered 1 Chronicles 29:15–16: "For we are strangers before thee, and sojourners, as were all our fathers. . . . O LORD our God, all this store that we have prepared to build thee an house for thine holy name cometh of thine hand, and is all thine own." Belle found new strength from God to enter the church, and the congregation welcomed mother and son to their meetings.

As she continued to attend the Methodist meetings, Belle learned to tell all her troubles to Jesus. At one meeting, when she said a devil was after her, apparently meaning it quite literally, a Methodist brother advised her that if she called on Jesus, the devil would leave. Recalling this once, Belle said in her droll style, "And I told him, I knowed that all the time, but I didn't happen to think of it before."

Methodists were members of a new, populist denomination that was disdained by the more formal, elite Dutch Reformed. who tended to dominate the area. Kingston

Methodist, like many Methodist churches elsewhere, welcomed blacks. It had established a Sunday school for them as early as 1811. By the mid-1820s, Methodists had built their first church in Kingston, a primitive building of rough-hewn timber. The Methodists emphasized direct, personal experience with God; they witnessed and spoke without preparation; and they liked to sing—all of which suited Belle. A member of the Dumont family recalled Belle during this period as a "roaring Methodist." Belle took her children with her to church as often as possible.

At one of these church meetings, Belle met Miss Geer, a vacationing schoolteacher from New York City. While Miss Geer related well to Belle, the schoolteacher was struck by Peter's inquisitive nature and bright mind. She told Belle, "There are many jobs available in New York City and a world of opportunities for Peter in terms of his education. You should consider moving to New York when you can."

The idea opened Belle's mind to all kinds of possibilities. After Freedom Day, many former slaves had moved to New York City, while others had taken jobs on the Erie Canal or found work in other cities. Why shouldn't she move to New York City? She might find a better-paying job and be able to save money for a home. Then as her children reached twenty-one and were freed by Dumont, they would have a place to live in New York City.

When Belle broached the subject with her daughters

Diana, Hannah, and Elizabeth, they encouraged her to take the opportunity for the sake of Peter. They promised to care for their younger sister, Sophia. Belle felt liberated just by being able to make such a decision without needing to get permission from a master.

At the end of the summer of 1829, Belle and Peter said a tearful good-bye to the rest of their family and left New Paltz. They promised to keep in touch with the Van Wageners, then boarded a boat to carry them down the Hudson River to New York City.

When the boat pulled into New York Harbor, Belle presented an imposing figure. She stood six feet tall and was dressed in a plain gray dress with a white bandanna tied around her head. Before leaving New Paltz, Belle had a cobbler make her first pair of shoes. Usually she walked barefoot or wore men's boots because her feet were size twelve.

Miss Geer met Belle and Peter at the docks with her carriage. As the carriage rolled over the cobblestone streets, Peter clung to his mother and looked wide-eyed at the new and interesting sights. The busy streets and masses of people amazed Belle, who had only known small-town life. She sat straight-backed in her seat and looked the picture of calmness and composure. In reality, she was extremely frightened. The sights out her window were very unfamiliar. The clutter and the noise of the city bombarded her senses and confused her. It was unlike anything that Belle had ever seen. People were everywhere and in constant motion. Some stood in groups on the sidewalk and talked while others were in carriages or on horseback. When their carriage passed some buildings that were several stories high, Belle looked up and felt dizzy.

For a few days, Belle settled into her new surroundings. Miss Geer had arranged for Belle to begin working for the Whitings, the Garfield family, and later a prominent newspaper family. She enrolled Peter in a navigation school, which captured his interest in ships and sailing.

Through wandering around the neighborhoods, Belle began to learn her way around New York City. She often listened as people stood talking outside a shop or market. Before long, she learned that Five Points was the poorest section of the city. Widowed mothers with children and people down on their luck lived with the murderers, thieves, and prostitutes. Thousands of Irish immigrants flooded the city on an almost-daily basis. Belle saw how many of these new arrivals didn't have a job or place to live, so they crowded into dirty conditions that were worse than any night she'd spent in the Hardenberghs' cellar. *Why do free people decide to live like this?* she wondered.

Belle was handicapped because she didn't know how to read and write. She could not read the Bible, even though she believed that knowing the Bible was important. She could not guide Peter in his schoolwork at the navigation school. She did not know for a long time that Peter was only pretending to attend school. Belle had a bank account but could not read the bank records.

There is some evidence that friends tried to teach

Belle to read and write. Much later in her life, Belle said, "When I was liberated, there was an attempt made to educate me, but I could not get beyond the ABCs."

While Belle remained illiterate, she became a zealous Methodist. Before long, Belle discovered the long-standing free black community in New York, and she proudly joined their growing ranks. One day, Belle was told that whites and blacks worshiped in separate services at the Methodist church on John Street. To see it for herself, Belle visited the Mother Zion African Methodist Episcopal (AME) Church.

The AME church was the oldest African American organization in the United States. African Americans Richard Allen and Absalom Jones started the church after they were not permitted to worship with white members at St. George's Church in Philadelphia. Born a slave in Delaware, Allen was ordained a minister in 1799 and started the African Methodist EpiscopalChurch. He became its first bishop. To Belle's surprise and pleasure, she learned that Allen had ordained a woman minister, Jarena Lee, in 1824, and that Lee had even preached at Mother Zion's in New York. During her days in New York City, Belle was a loved member of this AME church and known for her spirit-filled prayers and original hymns.

According to a newsman who befriended Belle later, she believed what she was taught at the church; she outprayed and outpreached her fellows; she "became the means of converting some by her zeal, and was much respected." According to a white Methodist leader at the time, "the influence of her speaking was miraculous." Still Belle wanted to learn, especially from whites.

Once Belle offered to pray with a black woman who declined her offer; hurt, Belle went away weeping. Blacks wanted to hear great preachers, Belle explained, not ignorant ones like herself. Finding only limited satisfaction in preaching and praying, Belle, at about the age of thirty-three, was looking for someone to guide her, someone educated and who seemed to be in touch with God.

One Sunday a few months later, a man and a woman approached Belle after the AME services. The woman told her, "I am your sister Sophia, and this is your brother Michael. We are also the children of Mau Mau Brett and Baumfree. Some of our friends told us that you worshiped in this church, so we came here to find you." Incredible joy filled Belle as she was reunited with one of her older sisters and with the brother who had been snatched away on a sled as a child and sold into slavery.

The three siblings spent the entire day talking and catching up on their lives. Sophia was living in New-burgh, New York, while Michael had moved to New York City. Belle asked about their other sister, Nancy, who was sold at the same time as Michael.

"Nancy lived here in New York," Michael said. "In fact, she attended Mother Zion until her recent death." Then Michael described Nancy's appearance, and Belle shrieked with surprise and delight. Nancy had been one of the elderly mothers in the congregation. Belle had prayed alongside Nancy at the altar, and they had sung hymns together. The women had never known that they were sisters.

Years later, when Belle told the story of her life for a biographer, she explained with tears running down her cheeks, "We met, and at the time I was struck with a peculiar feeling when I touched her hand. The bony hardness felt so much like my own hands, but I didn't know Nancy was my sister. Now looking back, I see how much Nancy looked like our mother."

As Michael, Sophia, and Belle sat in a park together, they cried at how slavery had torn apart their family and their lives. "What is this slavery?" Belle exclaimed. "It can do such terrible things!"

Miss Geer continued to encourage Belle and Peter as they adjusted to life in New York City. She invited Belle to join her and some others who went into the Five Points area of New York where they told people about the changing power of Jesus Christ. A few times, Belle went with the small group of Christians into this poor section of the city. They greeted people on the street corners and sang hymns in the street. But Belle wondered why they did it. *The people who live in Five Points need food, decent houses, and clothing,* she thought. *There must be another way to show Christ's love.*

When Belle heard about the Magdalene Asylum, a shelter for homeless women, she offered to help out. Elijah Pierson ran the shelter at a large gray house on Bowery Hill. Unknown to Belle and his followers,

Pierson was a religious fake. Several years earlier, Pierson had been a merchant, but after an intensely spiritual experience, Pierson had become religious. The Piersons sold their home and started the Magdalene Asylum for homeless women. He claimed to run the Magdalene Asylum with instructions directly from God. Such a claim wasn't hard for Belle to believe because she felt God directly guided her decisions and life. Belle liked Pierson and agreed to work part-time and often participated in his religious services.

The Piersons became noted for their unusual religious practices, such as going without food or water for four days or longer while holding prayer sessions. They hoped that such long fasts would win favor in God's eyes. The couple encouraged others like Belle to follow their example.

Belle believed that Pierson was a man with great spiritual powers whom God had selected to relieve the plight of the poor in New York City. When Belle learned about fasting from Pierson, she resolved to try it so that it would bring what Pierson called "light to her spirit." But going without food was dangerous for someone who worked hard physically like Belle. Determined to become enlightened, Belle went three days and nights without food or water. On the fourth day when she got up, Belle was so weak that she fell to the floor. She didn't want to appear a glutton in God's eyes, so she only ate dry bread and water. She resolved not to attempt to fast again. As she said, "I did get light, but it was all in my body and not in my mind—and this lightness in my body lasted for a long time."

Pierson's wife, Sara, discovered the dangers of fasting too late. After a prolonged fast in 1830, she died. Her illness and death deeply affected her husband. Pierson was so convinced that God had given him supernatural powers that he called his followers together and attempted to bring Sara back to life.

When their attempt to bring back his wife failed, Elijah Pierson again claimed that he had been given divine powers and God had chosen him to start a kingdom of God on earth. The vision came while Pierson was riding on a bus on June 20, 1830. He began to call himself by the title of Prophet and told people, "God has called me Elijah the Tishbite and said, 'Gather to Me all the members of Israel at the foot of Mount Carmel.' " Pierson understood the words to mean that he should gather people at the Magdalene Asylum on Bowery Hill.

One Sunday morning, Belle answered the front door of the asylum. She was startled to see a long-bearded figure in a flowing robe. The man asked to see Elijah the Tishbite and told Belle, "I am Matthias. I am God the Father and have the power to do all things." His eyes were piercing, and Belle thought the man might be an angel. He wore his beard long because Matthias believed that no man who shaved could be a true Christian. In actuality, Matthias was a middle-aged hustler named Robert Matthews who had arrived in the city with a new scheme to steal money from people.

Born from Scottish ancestry in Washington County, New York, Matthias called himself various names such as a Jewish teacher or a prophet of the Lord or the Spirit of Jesus or "Matthias, the twelfth and last of the Apostles." He made it clear that he believed that he had the power to heal the sick, to forgive sins, and to punish the wicked. He rejected the fasting that Pierson promoted but abstained from wine and pork and was inclined to be a vegetarian.

Matthias also believed in reincarnation, saying that when good people died, their spirits entered the bodies of the living. Before coming to New York, he had invaded churches to preach, sometimes interrupting the pastor, and had been jailed. Now he simply preached on the streets.

In Albany, New York, Matthias had a wife and children. His wife, who believed him to be honest, nevertheless opposed his calling himself a Jew. She rejected his beliefs and declined to travel with him on his trips to convert the world. For long periods Matthias abandoned his wife and family.

Within months, Pierson and Matthias had become partners in a wicked plan of deceit. Pierson now claimed to be John the Baptist on earth and Matthias was God on earth. Matthias preached to people, "Ours is the mustard seed kingdom, which is to spread throughout the entire earth. Our creed is truth but no one can discover truth unless he comes clean into the church."

Belle listened to these men, and their smooth talk

convinced her that they were exactly who they claimed—God and John the Baptist.

The community that Pierson and Matthias started was called "The Kingdom." The two men founded their community on a farm owned by a married couple, Benjamin and Ann Folger. The farm was located near the Hudson River, about thirty miles north of New York City. Every member of the Kingdom donated all their worldly possessions and money. Pierson and Matthias were the only ones who controlled the finances, and they didn't have to report on how the funds were used. Since Belle didn't have much money, the men accepted her into the group on the basis that she would do the washing, ironing, cooking, and cleaning. For her hard work, Belle would gain the privilege of worshiping with the others in the Kingdom.

Nothing indicates that Belle brought her children to the Kingdom, even though other children were there. Pierson brought his youngest daughter, Elizabeth, age twelve; the Folgers brought two children, ages five and ten; later, Matthias brought four of his children, too.

At the farm, Belle did more than her share of the work. Besides cooking and cleaning, she helped care for the sick. In his Kingdom, Matthias preached and prayed, but scarcely allowed anyone else to do so—and certainly not women. He believed the correct role of women was to be obedient and stay at home. Although Belle was accustomed to preaching and praying in public, she seemed to find Matthias's frank insistence on the lower role of women acceptable. She was fascinated with Matthias's openness, and she could not believe that anyone so open could have an evil side to his nature.

Matthias insisted on being called the head of the Kingdom household. He expected to be called Father. Under his firm authority, the house was clean and orderly. At meals, he presided and served all the food. All of the members drank water, but Matthias drank from a silver goblet while the rest of the group drank from ordinary glass tumblers. Except for Matthias' fine clothes and carriage, their lives were generally plain, so their expenses were not great. Matthias gave orders to everyone, including Pierson, as if they were his servants. He also whipped his own children, including his daughter who had just been married.

Once he whipped Belle when she was sick. Matthias had given her permission to rest in the kitchen by the fire. When he came into the kitchen, he found one of his sons in some mischief, which he corrected. Belle tried to intercede for the son, and Matthias quickly lashed her with his cowhide, saying, "Shall a sick devil undertake to dictate to me?"

Belle didn't rebel against Matthias's authority. She accepted Matthias as ordained by God and was devoted to him.

Gradually it became apparent that Matthias, once he secured money from his followers, had a taste for spending it. When in New York, he dressed elegantly and drove on Broadway in a fine carriage. Or he slowly walked along the Battery with great dignity. With the money from his especially wealthy supporters, Matthias appeared with a green frock coat heavily embroidered with gold, a linen shirt with wristbands fringed with lace, a crimson silk sash around his waist, well-polished Wellington boots, and a gold watch. One editor recalled, "Matthias's appearance was striking and calculated to attract notice."

Sometimes Matthias would preach to the crowd that gathered at his front door, but as one newspaper reported later, "Whenever Matthias would become irritated with Belle in regards to household or other matters, he would remain at home and preach to her the whole day."

One day, the family of one of Matthias's followers brought a charge against him for lunacy. The police came to the house and roughly arrested Matthias. They stripped him, took his money, and cut off his beard. Matthias submitted to the treatment, but Belle offered some resistance to the police. One of the family members who brought the charges against Matthias struck Belle. The police continued to try to put Belle outside of the house, but she continued to return inside.

A crowd that included Christian clergymen gathered to cheer on the arrest and the rough treatment of Matthias. Some people in the crowd called out that Matthias was an impostor. Belle didn't believe them. She said later, "I didn't see anything humane about this treatment nor the religion that suggested it." The experience drew her closer to Matthias.

The police took Matthias to the Bellevue prison and

put him in the section for the insane; but Pierson, supported by Belle, arranged for Matthias's release.

From the first, the members of the Kingdom washed and kissed each other's feet, in accordance with biblical tradition and as an act of humility. Later one newspaper reporter made fun of this practice and focused on Belle saying, "One brother, who believed in doing and not talking, proceeded in humility to kiss the foot of the colored cook."

For a while, the members of the community lived in peace and harmony. Then Matthias began to exert complete control over the community, and his unusual teaching caused a great deal of tension in the group. He claimed that every person had a soul that needed to have a spiritual bond with his or her marriage partner. According to Matthias, if their souls matched, then the people should be married and have sexual relations.

Matthias determined that Ann Folger's soul didn't match her husband's soul. Then Matthias issued a divorce (even though he didn't have any legal authority to do so) and married Ann Folger himself. Benjamin Folger was extremely upset over these actions and began to feud with Matthias.

Belle began to tire of the constant bickering and strange religious rituals. She decided that Matthias and Pierson didn't deserve her trust and confidence. While she had no proof of their dishonesty, Belle decided that she didn't want any part of deceiving others, so she prepared to leave.

In August 1834, Belle returned to New York City, and with Miss Geer's help, she got her old job back with the Whiting family. Back in the city, Belle learned that not only had Peter dropped out of school and hired out as a coachman for one of Miss Geer's friends, but also that Peter was running around with a rough crowd. This disturbing turn of events gave her further incentive to break her relationship with the Kingdom.

Meanwhile at the Folger farm, Pierson, who had started to have seizures before moving from New York City, began to develop even more serious physical problems. By the summer of 1834, he had become so weak that he often stayed in bed. In accordance with Pierson's and Matthias's beliefs, the community did not call a doctor. Matthias believed that diseases were caused by the presence of devils, and that he had the power to cast them out and prevent any members of the Kingdom from dying.

Belle made a brief trip to the farm to gather her possessions and tell the leaders that she was leaving. Suddenly, Pierson stiffened and collapsed on the floor. By the next morning, he was dead.

Pierson's relatives and friends, as well as people in the neighborhood, raised questions about his death. They were already suspicious of the Kingdom and Matthias, who insisted that "devils" were anyone who disagreed with his doctrines, which included nearly everyone in the neighborhood. Suspecting murder, the local coroner asked doctors to examine Pierson's body. A jury investigated and enjoyed the opportunity to poke into the affairs of the Kingdom.

The trial turned into a media circus, and every day the newspapers featured stories about the strange religious group and their two leaders who had used money for their own greedy desires. When the newspapers described the strange worship practices, Belle felt betrayed and hurt. These articles told about cheating, lying, and other evil practices such as adultery. She was as shocked as anyone on the street about these matters. As the only black woman involved in the Kingdom, Belle's role was used to add drama to the stories. To Belle's dismay, the public found it hard to believe that she knew nothing about the strange practices.

In the aftermath of the trial, the Kingdom began to fall apart. Westchester County seized the Folgers' farm, forcing all of the members to move. Mrs. Folger decided to return to her husband, and the Folgers moved back to their house in New York City. Belle, along with Matthias and his children, moved in with the Folgers, although they were not welcome houseguests.

In September 1834, the Folgers, who were facing business losses and financial trouble, explained to Matthias that they could no longer afford to support the Kingdom. This led to a painful argument between the Folgers and Matthias. Then the Folgers, hoping that it would encourage Belle to leave, paid her twenty-five dollars as wages. This payment was against the Kingdom's policy that everyone served without wages. So, still loyal to Matthias, Belle turned over the money to him and made it clear that she wanted to stay with him. But Matthias returned the money to her.

The Folgers were also hoping to fend off Matthias, so they gave him $530 with the expectation, according to Belle, that he would use it carry out his dream of buying a farm in the West. By the end of September 1834, Matthias had left the Folger house and gone to Albany to prepare to move West.

Belle expected to go west with Matthias, even if it meant leaving her children behind. On the day that Matthias left the Folger house, Belle also left, taking her luggage with her. She assumed she left the Folgers on good terms.

Traveling north, Belle visited those of her children who were still at the Dumont estate in New Paltz, then took a steamboat up the Hudson River to Albany where she joined Matthias at his wife's house. While there, Belle was surprised to learn that the Folgers had brought charges against Matthias. The police were about to arrest him for stealing the $530 that Belle had understood the Folgers had given him. Confused and upset, Belle returned to New York City.

Once Matthias had left the city, the Folgers had complained to the police that he had obtained the money from them under false pretenses. The Folgers also circulated other charges and fed the suspicions of the community about the Kingdom. They charged that Matthias, with Belle's help, had murdered Pierson by serving him poisoned blackberries. Also the Folgers claimed that Matthias and Belle had tried to murder them by serving them poisoned coffee.

In response to these new charges, the police ordered that Pierson's body be taken out of its grave and reexamined by doctors. Although the doctors did not find any clear evidence of poison in the body, they found some unknown but "deadly" substance in it. Benjamin and Ann Folgers took advantage of the publicity and wrote a novel about their experiences, which was thinly based on fact. In this novel, the Folgers blamed a maid for introducing the evil in their holy community. In the story, this "black witch" murdered the leader of the organization, and the book detailed how the murder was accomplished. The public read the novel and believed the story was about Belle. Newspapers published excerpts from the novel and continued to spread the false story.

Gilbert Vale was a friend of Mr. Whiting, Belle's employer. Both men were journalists, and Whiting was convinced that Belle was incapable of any of the crimes that the Folgers had described. Vale was persuaded to take up Belle's cause; and in 1835, he published a pamphlet called, "Fanaticism: Its Source and Influence, Illustrated by the Simple Narrative of Isabella." The pamphlet gave Belle a chance to tell her story to the public. Vale suggested that Belle might sue the Folgers for their published lies, as well as sue the newspapers that had published the novel.

Years earlier, Belle had seen the power truth could have in the courtroom, so she took Vale's challenge and fought for her good name—the only valuable possession for a poor person. Her plan was simple. She returned to New Paltz and Kingston to gather character statements from her employers. Her old master John Dumont praised Belle as being "perfectly honest." Isaac Van Wagener described Belle as "a faithful servant, honest and industrious."

Finally, her most recent employer, Mrs. Whiting, wrote a glowing statement about Belle, saying, "I do state unequivocally that we never have had such a servant that did all her work so faithfully, and one in whom we could place such implicit confidence. In fact, we did, and do still believe her to be a woman of extraordinary moral purity."

Henry M. Western, a lawyer, advised Belle to prosecute the Folgers for slander, that it was the only way to clear her name. Vale reported Belle to have replied, "I have got the truth and I know it, and I will crush them with the truth."

The murder trial of Matthias finally came to the courts in April 1835. State Circuit Judge Charles H. Ruggles presided. Before Ruggles had become a judge, he had helped Belle get her son back from Alabama, and he thought well of her.

As a trial lawyer, Western declared that his principal witness was "Isabella, a black woman," even though he knew that many whites would find any black witness hard to believe. Belle, Western explained, was in court and ready to give her evidence, but as her character had been questioned, he wished to support it by the testimony of some witnesses who had not yet arrived at the court. To give Western more time, the court postponed the trial until the next day.

When the trial proceeded, Matthias pronounced a curse of God on the jury, for which he was examined for insanity but declared sane. Doctors testified that they had not clearly found poison in Pierson's stomach. Lawyer Western argued that Pierson had died of epilepsy. The prosecution could offer no substantial evidence that Pierson had been murdered, nor that Pierson, even if he had received adequate medical care, would not have died soon from epilepsy anyway. Judge Ruggles advised the jury that in the absence of adequate evidence, Matthias should be acquitted. The jury promptly agreed.

Belle believed that justice had triumphed, but she was disappointed that neither her character witnesses nor she herself had been called to testify. She wanted a chance to tell her story.

The district attorney, sympathetic with the public's feeling that Matthias was a rogue who should be convicted of something, immediately charged Matthias with assaulting his own daughter. The pretty young Mrs. Charles Laisdell asked the court to drop this charge, but her husband, Charles Laisdell, insisted that the case go forward. The daughter testified that her father had whipped her with his cowhide across her shoulders and arms because he had intended to find her another husband, and she had refused to accept.

Judge Ruggles instructed the jury that because Mrs. Laisdell was legally married, Matthias could not legally whip her. The jury convicted Matthias of assaulting his daughter. The judge sentenced him to three months in prison for this conviction, plus one more month for contempt of court for cursing the jury. In sentencing him, Judge Ruggles called Matthias a "barefaced impostor" who had tried to tell his daughter her marriage was void.

Newspapers splashed the story of Matthias and his Kingdom over their pages. At least one newspaper in New York and one in Albany devoted its whole front page to a report about the murder trial. The *New York Times* found it intriguing that a wealthy and educated family like the Folgers had submitted themselves to Matthias's command. The *Albany Argus* called Matthias "the most notable impostor, at least, of all modern times." The *New York Sun* circulated the rumor that Matthias had had one wife for each day of the week.

After coming out of prison, Matthias moved west without Belle. It was not clear at this time whether or not Belle wanted to go with Matthias.

In November 1835, Matthias visited Joseph Smith, the founder of the Mormon church, at the Mormon settlement in Kirtland, Ohio. Matthias identified himself as Joshua, a Jewish teacher; and Smith, since his curiosity was aroused, invited him to stay with him for several days. After listening to him at length, Smith figured out that he was, in fact, the notorious Matthias. Since Smith had decided Matthias was a murderer and that his doctrines were of the devil, he asked him to leave.

The suit Belle had brought against Benjamin Folger for slander soon came to trial. Her employer, Perez Whiting, testified that Folger, after charging that Belle had tried to help murder both Pierson and the Folgers, had admitted to Whiting that his charge was not true. Folger offered no defense, so Belle won, but again without having her opportunity to testify in court. The court awarded her $125 in damages plus costs.

Remarkably, this marked the second time that an illiterate black woman had taken a case to court and the second time that she had won. These two victories, along with her belief that Matthias had been justly acquitted of murder, apparently left her with an exalted respect for the law.

For Belle, little victory was in the money that she gained. Instead, she felt that for three years (from 1832 to 1835) she had wasted her life and time. In God's economy, however, these years were not wasted. Never again was Belle so easily taken in by fast-talking men who mistook honesty and sincerity for weakness. Her painful lessons had equipped her to face what life was soon to bring.

FIVE

Belle had won the fight of her life and had preserved her reputation, but in a different part of her life, a new battle was already brewing. According to Belle, her son Peter had "gone to seed." For a while, through using firm discipline, she had been able to keep Peter under control, but when she had moved to the Kingdom and left Peter in the city, he had dropped out of navigation school and also refused to attend grammar school.

The city around Peter was bursting with violence that, to the young boy, looked like great adventure. Instead of learning in the classroom, Peter wanted to hang out with his friends—mostly street thugs. Although only eleven years old, Peter was tall for his age, so the street boys accepted him into their group. He liked being with the older boys and stole things to win their approval.

Because Peter wasn't in school, his mother insisted

that he find work. Earlier, the boy had been working as a coachman for Mr. Jones. Then one day, Peter disappeared with Mr. Jones's best saddle. A few days later, Peter showed up for work again. He confessed that he had sold the saddle, then used the money for a good time with his friends. Miss Geer and Belle pleaded with Mr. Jones not to press charges against Peter. Mr. Jones allowed himself to be persuaded, but he fired Peter and turned him out on the streets.

For his mother and Miss Geer, Peter flashed his charming smile and promised never to steal again, but a day or two later, Peter had forgotten his promise. Throughout New York City, blacks and Irish competed for jobs during the day and fought for control of territory at night. Peter often got into these nighttime fights and would come home for Belle to patch his injuries. Each time, she would scold Peter and lecture him about fighting. Then Peter would plead for another chance to correct his wrongdoings. His promise never lasted more than a few days. Soon Peter was in trouble again.

Several times Peter got in trouble with the police, and they threw the boy into jail. On two different occasions, Belle asked for advances on her salary so she could pay Peter's fines and get him out of jail. She always believed in her son. Then Belle found Peter a job in a livery stable. Peter had to take care of the horses, rake out the stalls, and clean the harnesses and bridles. About half the time, Peter didn't go to work, and when he did, he fought with his boss. When Peter stole a bridle and sold it on the streets, the boss pressed charges against him.

Belle knew that she had lost control of her son. He was on a crash course with disaster, and she couldn't help him. The only way that Peter could change would be from his own desire for help. So when the messenger came to tell Belle that Peter had been thrown into the Tombs, New York's dreaded jailhouse, she refused to help. Because Belle had warned Peter over and over, she decided to "give Peter up to God."

The boy couldn't believe his mother's reaction. Belle had always been there for him. Even after Peter had spent an entire day in jail, his mother had not come. He was so frightened at the idea of staying in the jailhouse that he created a clever plan. Sometimes Peter used the name of Peter Williams. In the city, there was a minister by the same name, so Peter sent a message of help to his "namesake." For some reason, the elderly Williams decided to help the boy, but first he visited with his mother. Together Williams and Belle agreed that Peter needed discipline—and that the best place for that discipline was at sea as a sailor. They convinced the local judge to agree with their plan and sentence Peter to work as a sailor.

In August 1839, Peter signed up as a crew member aboard the *Zone of Nantucket*. A year later, Belle received a letter from her son, which Mrs. Whiting read to her.

> *My dear and beloved Mother,*
> *I take this opportunity to write to you and in-*
> *form you that I am well and in hopes for to find*

*you the same. I am got on board the same unlucky
ship* Zone *of Nantucket. I am sorry for to say
that I have been punished once severely, for shov-
ing my head in the fire for other folks. I would like
to know how my sisters are. I wish you would
write me an answer as soon as possible. I am your
son that is so far from home in the wide briny
ocean. Mother, I hope you do not forget me, your
dear and only son. I hope you all will forgive me
for all that I have done.*

> *Your son,*
> *Peter Van Wagener*

Belle dictated letters back to Peter. No one knows
what Belle wrote to Peter in these letters, but they were
likely about family, friends, and activities in the community. Many changes had taken place since Peter had
left New York City. In 1830, there were 13,976 blacks
who lived in the city. Although whites and blacks had
worked together to end slavery, now they competed
fiercely and sometimes violently for jobs, education,
and housing. Crime was widespread, and the government was corrupt. Belle saw the wickedness around her
and said, "The rich rob the poor and the poor rob one
another." Many of Peter's old friends were dead or in
jail, so she thanked God that her son had escaped such
an ending to his young life.

Belle didn't want to write Peter about the ugly side of
New York because her son had seen enough of that life

when he had lived there. So she told Peter about old Mary Washington, a servant of President Washington, who still sold fruits and vegetables at 79 John Street between Gold and Nassau Street. When the first president had died in 1799, Mary had put out a display in his memory, which she still maintained. She wanted his birthday to be a national holiday, and Belle agreed.

Every day Belle watched for letters from Peter. She missed him deeply. A second letter came, and then five months later—September 19, 1841—a third letter arrived. Peter told his mother how his ship had fallen on bad luck, but he was certain that his luck was about to change.

He wrote, "This is the fifth letter that I have wrote to you and have received no answer and it makes me uneasy. So pray write as quick as you can."

Belle stopped Mrs. Whiting as she was reading the letter and said, "I've written many letters to Peter and we've only received three from him. Why hasn't he received my letters?"

"Let's continue and see what additional information we learn," Mrs. Whiting encouraged.

The letter continued, "I should be home in fifteen months. I have not much to say, but tell me if you have been at home since I left or not. I want to know what sort of a time is at home. So write as soon as you can, won't you?"

Then Peter finished the letter with a poem that he had found or possibly written himself:

Notice when this you see, remember me,
and place me in your mind.
Get me to my home
that's in the far distant west,
To the scenes of my childhood,
that I like the best;
There the tall cedars grow,
and the bright waters flow,
Where my parents will greet me,
white man, let me go!
Let me go to the spot
where the cateract plays,
Where oft I have sported
in my boyish days;
And there is my poor mother,
whose heart ever flows,
At the sight of her poor child,
to her let me go. . .let me go!

The letter was signed, "Your only son, Peter Van Wagener."

Immediately Belle wrote Peter and told him about her dream to rent a house where the entire family could live together and share life. Months passed, but Belle never heard from Peter again. Many years later, she was told Peter's ship, the *Zone*, had returned to New York Harbor, but it had no crew member by the name of Peter Williams or Peter Van Wagener.

As Belle thought about her son, she remembered the

words of her mother, Mau Mau Brett: "Those are the same stars, and that is the same moon, that look down upon your brothers and sisters, and which they see as they look up at them, though they are ever so far away from us, and each other."

Belle always kept Peter's letters. Years later, she told her biographer, "I have no doubt. I feel sure that Peter has persevered and kept the resolve he made before he left home."

Often during the pitch-black of the night, Belle would look at the night sky and wonder if her children were seeing the same beautiful North Star. (For slaves, the North Star held a special meaning—it pointed to freedom.)

Years passed, and Belle continued to live and work in New York City for Mrs. Whiting. Soon it was 1843. All of Belle's daughters had grown up and married—even started their own families. When she thought about it, Belle was sad that she had not spent more time with her daughters as they had grown up, but she could do little to change the past. Now she wondered how to make her future better.

As Belle thought about New York City, she began to realize it was a dangerous place for blacks. Throughout the streets, slave catchers roamed and searched for blacks who had escaped slavery in the South. Sometimes free slaves were captured along with runaway slaves. Then they were smuggled out of the city and into slavery. Also as blacks and European immigrants competed fiercely for jobs, some blacks faced severe discrimination and became victims of racial violence.

After living fourteen years in or near New York City, Belle decided that New York was no longer the place for her. She felt it was "a wicked city"—a "Sodom." She became convinced that she herself had been robbing the poor because she had been taking on extra jobs that she did not really need. She became convicted that she had been unfeeling, selfish, and wicked.

In addition, Belle believed that everything she had undertaken in the city had failed. She had tried to preach, but the blacks, whom she especially wanted to reach, had rejected her. She had tried to help build the kingdom of God on earth through Matthias's community, but it had blown up into a scandal and damaged her good name. She had attempted to save enough money for her own home but had failed. She had tried to raise her son, Peter, to be honest and industrious like herself, but he had fallen into stealing and been imprisoned several times.

Because of her uneasy feelings about herself, Belle decided that she must leave the city; but for some time, she didn't say anything to anyone about her plans. She was afraid that if her children and friends knew about it, they would object and make things unpleasant. Belle was, at this time, about forty-six years old.

Belle decided to become a traveling evangelist. Although it was unusual for women to preach, there were several black women in the Northeast who had become traveling evangelists, such as Rebecca Jackson and Jarena

Lee from Philadelphia and Julia Foote from Boston, Massachusetts, and Binghamton, New York. Before becoming traveling evangelists, each of these women had gained experience as preachers among the Methodists. Several of them had become widowed or otherwise separated from their husbands, so they were free from any conventional constraints on their preaching. Jarena Lee received help in finding places to preach from Bishop Richard Allen of the African Methodist Episcopal Church; but, as far as it is known, Belle didn't receive any assistance in her desire to become a traveling evangelist. She left without the promise of support from any church or denomination, and with no one advising her.

When she began to dream about a new life away from New York City, Belle understood that her perspective as a freed slave, a mother, and a devout Christian gave her a different viewpoint about human rights and spiritual well-being. She wanted to tell others about her experiences. As Belle prayed, a powerful voice told her, "You have a mission to the needy and the oppressed."

During one of her times in prayer, Belle thought she received a message from God, "Go east." The words troubled her, and she wondered if she should follow them, but they came again, "Go east." Belle made a decision to follow the Lord to the East—wherever He took her.

For any woman to just wander and speak as the way opened was both unusual and dangerous, but Belle believed that God had called her to leave her unhappy life in New York, begin a dangerous mission, and speak for Him. One thing still bothered her though: her name. The name that she had been given as a slave seemed inappropriate for a person beginning a new life as God's pilgrim. She wanted a new name for a free woman.

Calling on God for help in selecting a name, Belle remembered Psalm 39:12: "Hear my prayer, O LORD, and give ear unto my cry. . .for I am a stranger with thee, and a sojourner, as all my fathers were." To Belle, Sojourner was a good name for someone whom God had called to travel up and down the land, showing the people their sins and being a sign to them. The name also reminded Belle of the holy people described in the Bible who traveled to foreign countries and preached the Word of God. When Sojourner began her journey, she felt like her travels would model the great prophets from the Old Testament.

On June 1, 1843, as the first light shone over the horizon, Belle was already awake and stuffing her few dresses into an old pillowcase. At last the day of her departure had arrived. About an hour before she left, she informed the Whitings, where she had been working as a live-in domestic, that she was quitting. The Whitings were stunned that Belle was leaving and inquired where she would be staying.

"You're crazy, Belle," Mrs. Whiting said. "We need you here, and this is your home. Why travel to the East?"

But Belle could not be stopped. "The Spirit calls me there and I must go. I'm going to find a new home. . .and with a new name. I'm gone forever! The Lord is going to give me a new home," she told them, "and I am going away." Then Belle explained to Mrs. Whiting that she had taken the name of "Sojourner." Because Belle was traveling, Mrs. Whiting understood that Sojourner was an appropriate name. With those words, Belle flung her pillowcase of belongings across her shoulder and said, "Farewell, friends. I must be about my Father's business."

First, Belle walked to the ferry that was going to Brooklyn. She paid twenty-five cents for the crossing and continued walking toward Long Island. After nearly seventeen years since she'd escaped from slavery, Belle was once again traveling—except this time she truly felt free. In her customary style, Belle left New York City and never looked back.

By evening, she had walked well out of the city. Stopping at a Quaker farm, Sojourner asked for a drink of water. The woman gave it to her and asked for her name.

"My name is Sojourner," she replied with firmness.

But the first name wasn't enough for the woman. "Sojourner what?" she asked.

"My name is Sojourner," the former slave answered and continued on her trip. But the woman's question continued to nag at her. *Only slaves don't have a last name,* she thought. *Just like my new first name came from God, I'll ask Him for a last name.*

Throughout her life, Belle had always been Hardenbergh's Belle, Dumonts' Belle—always with her master's names. In prayer, Sojourner remembered another Bible verse, John 8:32: "And ye shall know the truth, and the truth shall make you free."

"I've only got one master now—the God of the Universe and His name is Truth. My name is Sojourner Truth," she said to herself, "because from this day I will walk in the light of His truth." It seemed a perfect name for one of God's pilgrims.

Years later, Sojourner explained to Harriet Beecher Stowe how her name had changed. "When I left the house of bondage, I left everything behind. I wasn't going to keep anything from Egypt on me, so I went to the Lord and asked Him to give me a new name. The Lord gave me the name Sojourner, because I was to travel up and down the land, showing people their sins, and being a sign unto them. Afterwards I told the Lord I wanted another name, because everybody else had two names; and the Lord gave me Truth, because I was to declare the truth to the people."

Sojourner also explained her change of name in terms of her slavery. She had been born as a slave and sold and resold four different times and known by as many names. Each time, Belle had taken the name of her slave master; but after slavery ended, she took the name Truth.

SIX

"Go east," was Sojourner's only direction from God, so she continued walking east across Long Island. She preached in the farms and villages that she passed. These white farmers stopped their work to listen to Sojourner. They were enthralled with her powerful speaking voice and manners. To their amazement, she seemed to know every word in the Bible even though she was illiterate.

As Sojourner traveled, she was often invited to stay with people who gathered to hear her speak. To repay their acts of kindness, she washed their clothes and scrubbed their floors. Throughout Long Island, word spread about the fiery preacher.

One evening Sojourner walked to a large outdoor religious meeting. Hundreds of families were camped in wagons and tents, so she stayed the night and all the next day. The people ate, sang, prayed, and listened to speakers. The experience reminded Sojourner of the joyous days of Pinxter. Everyone seemed so happy and yet very spiritual.

Wearing her black Quaker dress and white shawl, one afternoon Sojourner approached the group and asked if she could speak to them. She climbed the platform, and the people gathered to hear her speak. A black woman as a speaker was unusual, so their curiosity quieted them. Clearly this was no ordinary woman, because Sojourner stood tall, strong-boned, and proud.

Sojourner began to speak in a deep melodious voice, "Well, children, I speaks to God and God speaks to me." As she paused, a murmur spread throughout the crowd. Standing in the late afternoon sunshine, talking about God's love, glory, and protection, the black woman must have looked like she came from another world. She concluded her message with a hymn, "In my trials, Lord, walk with me. In my trials, Lord, walk with me. When my heart is almost breaking, Lord, walk with me. . . ."

The group sang along with Sojourner and begged her for another song. So she sang a song that she'd learned from blacks who had fled the South to freedom in New York:

> *Sometimes I feel like a motherless child,*
> *Sometimes I feel like a motherless child,*
> *Sometimes I feel like a motherless child*
> *A long way from home,*
> *A long way from home.*

After this introduction to many different people in the area, Sojourner traveled and spoke from meeting to meeting. People began to whisper, "It must be Sojourner Truth," whenever she appeared at a religious meeting in a new neighborhood.

Once, someone asked Sojourner to speak about her life as a slave. It marked the first time for her to speak to such a large group of white people about her background, but after a prayer and a hymn, she began.

"Children, slavery is a evil thing," Sojourner said. "They sell children away from their mothers, and then dare the mothers to cry about their loss. What kind of men can do such an evil thing?"

A murmur of agreement went through the crowd, and Sojourner could see heads nodding while listening with respect. "My mother and father had eleven other children besides me. Some of my brothers and sisters I've never met because they were sold off before I was even born. But my poor Mau Mau Brett never stopped crying for them."

The audience was held captive as Sojourner told the story of her brother and sister being sold from the Hardenbergh estate, then later of her meeting her brother and another sister in New York.

Soon word spread throughout the region that she was an inspirational speaker with a stirring message. Whenever she arrived at a camp meeting, people rushed to greet her. After people heard her speak, they were often so filled with emotion that they cried or cheered.

During the early days of her speaking, Sojourner was amazed that white people would sit still and listen to anything that she said. Later, her goal for speaking became clearer. Throughout her life, she had been a victim of oppression. She had been despised because of her race and ignored because she was a woman. Now at age forty-six, she was dedicated to eliminating human suffering and speaking out against slavery. To speak against slavery became the central focus of her ministry.

Once in her travels, Sojourner came across a temperance meeting. She contributed to the meeting by helping to concoct some New York dishes of food to the satisfaction of everyone in attendance. Temperance, or the abstinence of using alcoholic beverages, became a subject that she was also comfortable speaking about. Her experience with the Methodists and with Pierson and Matthias prepared her to be comfortable speaking about this social cause.

During her travels, Sojourner stayed with whoever offered her food and lodging. Usually she found the poor, not the rich, made such offers. She did not seem afraid to live this way. If she needed money, then she stopped and did domestic work for a while.

Sojourner believed that the world was wicked; often she would say that it would look much better if we could see it right side up. She began to denounce the foolishness of following the crowd—a theme that she later developed in her preaching. During her travels, she attended evangelical meetings; and if the opportunity was offered, she spoke, prayed, and sang. Sometimes she held meetings of her own, or friends that she met through her travels arranged the meetings. As she later explained, "I found many true friends of Jesus with whom I could have communion."

Occasionally Sojourner attended the meetings of the followers of William Miller, or the Second Adventists. She felt somewhat uncomfortable with these meetings. They expected Christ to appear very soon and send fire to destroy the wicked. Sojourner felt they were too excited and fearful. In her talks with them, she tried to calm down their opinions. She believed that if people had faith, they could withstand any punishing fire that God might send into their lives. Although she was a Christian, she didn't agree with the practices of every group that labeled itself as Christian.

The theme of her speeches during these days was, "God's mercy will be shown to those who show mercy." The crowd marveled at this simple black woman speaker. She couldn't read, yet she could flawlessly quote scripture word for word and then apply it in an appropriate manner. For years, Sojourner had heard passages of the Bible and committed them to memory—solely through listening.

The sincerity of her message combined with the simplicity of her language and the courage of her convictions. Many people began to seek out Sojourner Truth as a speaker for their meetings. The farmers left their fields to hear her tell stories about when she was beaten for not understanding English. They laughed and cried as they heard her personal stories about life as a slave and the poor treatment that she had received as a free woman of color.

Sojourner continued to wander from place to place throughout the area and speak to anyone who would listen. Eventually she decided that she should follow God's call and move to another area. She took a ship across Long Island Sound and walked on through Connecticut and Massachusetts. Wherever she went, people flocked to hear her preach.

When winter came, Sojourner was ready to settle down for a while. For some time, she had been in the region of Springfield, Massachusetts. She looked for a quiet place where a worn traveler could rest.

After several months of traveling, she arrived in Northampton, a town located along the Connecticut River in the heart of Massachusetts. Her friends described her as a "commanding figure" with a dignified manner. She "hushed every trifler into silence," and "whole audiences were melted into tears by her touching stories."

While in Northampton, Sojourner visited the Northampton Association of Education and Industry, a cooperative community that operated a silkworm farm and made silk. She was impressed with how the people worked together.

The Northampton Association had been founded in 1842 and was led by two advocates of the abolition of slavery, Samuel L. Hill, an ex-Quaker, and George Benson, who was William Lloyd Garrison's brother-in-law. Garrison, who edited an abolitionist weekly newspaper in Boston, was a frequent visitor. In the eyes of some people, Garrison was the leader of the anti-slavery movement. This tall, gaunt-faced man with gentle eyes made angry speeches. He said, "Prejudice against color is rebellion against God."

When only twenty-three, Garrison had committed his life to ending slavery. In 1832, he'd formed the New England Anti-Slavery Society, which was the first to call for the immediate emancipation of all slaves. A year later, Garrison was in Philadelphia when the American Anti-Slavery Society was formed. Garrison's newspaper, the *Liberator,* inspired thousands in the abolitionist movement—especially the community at Northampton.

As a young man, Garrison had spent time in prison for his beliefs. Now as an adult, his belief in the wrongness of slavery never wavered. The front page of the *Liberator* had the opinion of the editor on its masthead: "No union with slaveholders."

Hill and Benson had heard about Sojourner Truth from friends and asked her to stay in their community at Northampton. Although these leaders were nothing like Matthias and Pierson, Sojourner was cautious before getting involved with them too quickly. Since her experience with the Kingdom, she had avoided any weird religious practices. Whenever she was with such a group, she would say with characteristic wit, "The Lord might come, move all through the camp, and go away again; and they'd never know it because of all the noise and commotion." Then she scolded them saying, "Here you are talking about being changed in a twinkling of an eye. If the Lord should come, He'd change you to nothing, for there is nothing in you."

Despite her uneasy feelings about a community life-style, Sojourner stayed in Northampton. She was attracted to the group because of their spirit of fellowship and idealism. They were a friendly haven for leading abolitionists. Her days at Northampton turned into the perfect training ground for her work as an abolitionist and feminist.

One of the frequent visitors at the community was Wendell Phillips. Sojourner learned that Phillips was called "Abolition's Golden Trumpet" because of his powerful speaking abilities. In fact, Phillips had drawn Sam Hill, one of the Northampton cofounders, into the abolitionist movement.

Another distinguished speaker was Parker Pillsbury, who visited the community on a regular basis. When Sojourner first heard Pillsbury, she was intimidated by this big, red-bearded man whose booming voice shook the chandeliers. He had earned a reputation for being an uncompromising abolitionist. Often during the meetings, Pillsbury wore a particular torn frock coat and told about how the coat had been ripped off his back by a pro-slavery mob. He said, "If they'd caught me, they would have ripped my head off, but I would still have gone on talking against slavers!"

Another person who Sojourner met at Northampton was David Ruggles, who also lived in the community. Both had spent many years in New York City but had never met. While at Northampton, they became good friends.

Ruggles had been born free in Norwich, Connecticut, but had worked most of his life in New York for the abolitionist movement. As a writer and editor, he fought slavery legally by donating his skills to the quarterly magazine, *The Mirror of Liberty*. In private, Ruggles served as secretary for the underground New York Vigilance Committee, which illegally helped runaway slaves escape. Along with his friend William Sill, Ruggles is credited with helping more than six hundred fugitive slaves while serving as conductors on the Underground Railroad.

While living in New York City, Ruggles had gone blind and would have undoubtedly ended up living on the streets, but for the help of his friends at Northampton. In the community, Ruggles experimented with hydrotherapeutic treatment, which he credited for helping him partially regain his sight. He continued his research, and in 1846, Ruggles opened a water-cure institute at Northampton. His success as a hydrotherapist was validated as people began to call him "doctor" even though he had never had formal medical training.

The children in the Northampton community loved Ruggles because he could tell stories about the escape of slaves with great excitement and adventure. He especially liked to tell stories about runaway slaves, like his friend Frederick Douglass.

Douglass was another frequent visitor to the Northampton community. He became an active member of the abolitionist movement and gained a reputation for outstanding speaking. In fact, his voice and perfect diction was so respected that it put him at a disadvantage. Southerners began to spread rumors that Douglass had never been a slave. To prove he wasn't a phony, Frederick wrote his autobiography in 1845, which gave names, dates, and events relevant to his life. While Sojourner couldn't read *Narrative of Frederick Douglass,* someone in Northampton read the book aloud to her.

Still a runaway, Douglass could have been recaptured and returned to the South in accordance with the Fugitive Slave Law of 1793. So for a while, Douglass left the United States and only returned when his freedom had been secured by abolitionists in England.

Douglass never forgot his old friend Ruggles and his help in the Underground Railroad. Whenever Douglass was in the area, he stopped to visit. Frederick Douglass was the only black representative in the Anti-Slavery Society. Other blacks were involved in different abolitionist organizations. Garrison and Douglass pushed the society to seek peaceful solutions to the slavery problems, but other blacks disagreed with this approach.

At the 1843 National Negro Convention in Buffalo, New York, twenty-seven-year-old Henry Highland Garnet, a Presbyterian minister, gave a stirring speech at the convention where seventy blacks attended. Garnet called for his black brothers to rise up in revolt and hold general strikes. He told the convention, "You had better all die—die immediately—than live as slaves and entail your wretchedness upon your posterity. If you would be free in this generation, here is your only hope. . . . But you are a patient people. You act as though you were made for the special use of those devils. You act as though your daughters were born to pamper the lusts of your masters and overseers. And worse than all, you tamely submit while your lords tear your wives from your embraces and defile them before your eyes. In the name of God, we ask, are you men? Where is the blood of your fathers? Has it run out of your veins? Awake! Awake! Millions of voices are calling you! Your dead fathers speak to you from their graves."

At the convention, Douglass answered Garnet's speech and called for moral persuasion rather than violence to end slavery. Back in Northampton, Sojourner listened as the newspaper accounts of this debate were read to her. As much as she despised and hated slavery, Sojourner could not support violence in any form, so she made a choice to stay in the Douglass-Garrison camp.

A few months after Sojourner had joined the Northampton community, she attended a nearby camp meeting held in the open fields. As often happened at the camp meetings, young rowdies invaded the meeting to amuse themselves. They hooted to interrupt the services and said they would burn the tents. The leaders of the meeting threatened the young men, but this only seemed to make them more agitated.

When the rowdies began to shake the tent where Sojourner was located, she caught the fear of the leadership and hid behind a trunk. If the men rushed inside the tent, she feared they would single her out and kill her, because she was the only black person present. Then, as she hid behind the trunk, Sojourner wondered whether a servant of the living God should hide. *Have I not faith enough to go out and quell that mob,* she wondered, *when I know it is written, "One [shall] chase a thousand, and two put ten thousand to flight"?*

Sojourner came out from hiding and invited a few of the camp meeting leaders to go outside with her and try to calm the mob. When the leaders refused, she went out by herself. She walked to a small rise of ground and started to sing one of her favorite hymns about the resurrection of Christ, "It Was Early in the Morning."

A few of the rioters gathered around her. During a pause in her singing, she asked them, "Why do you come about me with clubs and sticks? I am not doing harm to anyone."

Some of them answered, "We aren't going to harm you, old woman. We came to hear you sing." Others asked her to sing some more. Still others asked her to speak. Sojourner believed that some of these youths would be open to what she had to say, so she began to preach to them. From time to time, they asked questions, and she answered them. The group began to calm down.

As the number of young people listening to her grew, they asked her to stand on a nearby wagon so they could see her better. When she prepared to step up on a wagon, she asked them, "If I step up on it, will you tip it over?" Some of them replied that if anyone even tried such an act, they would knock that person down.

Sojourner mounted the wagon and continued talking and singing. Finally she asked them if she sang one more song, would they go away and leave the camp in peace. Some of them said they would. She asked them to say it louder, and they said it louder. She sang one more song, and then they began to move off, some of their leaders disciplining those who were reluctant to join them, until all of the mob had left the campgrounds.

After that incident, Sojourner decided never to run away again. She developed skill in handling rough crowds.

In 1846, Sojourner made a trip back to New Paltz so she could visit her daughter Diana, who continued working for the Dumonts. While Sojourner was visiting her daughter, she was glad to hear John Dumont, her former master, repent for his past actions. He told her, "Slavery is the wickedest thing in the world."

During her stay in the Northampton community, Sojourner heard lecturers who advocated that women should be given the same political and legal rights as men.

Recognizing that she and the women's rights speakers were kindred spirits, she decided to join their ranks and take on this new battle for freedom. After all, throughout her entire life, she had struggled with a double burden, being both a black and a woman in a society that imposed severe restrictions on both groups.

In the 1840s, a woman in the United States could not vote or hold political office. She was paid far less than a man for the same work. If she was fortunate enough to receive an education, usually she was taught in a separate classroom from the male students.

When a woman married, her property and earnings came under her husband's control. She could not initiate a divorce, but her husband could divorce her and she couldn't testify against him. Priests and ministers commonly told women that they were inferior to men.

The first significant opposition to this situation was organized by women such as Susan B. Anthony, Lucy Stone, and Angelina and Sarah Grimke, who had earlier worked to help abolish slavery in the North. From their participation in the abolitionist movement, these women had become experts at organizing meetings, collecting signatures for petitions, and speaking in public.

At Northampton, Sojourner was introduced to this growing movement for the equality of women. Olive Gilbert, an early feminist and a member of the Northampton society, read Sojourner an article in the *Liberator*, which reported on the first women's rights convention in Seneca Falls, New York, July 19–20, 1848. Douglass was the only man to play a prominent role in this convention for women's rights.

The convention had been planned by two women from New England, Elizabeth Cady Stanton and Lucretia Coffin Mott. During the second session of the convention, Stanton submitted a resolution that called for women to have the right to vote. William Lloyd Garrison disapproved of the resolution, and even Lucretia Mott differed with Stanton about pushing women's rights to this extent. Mott was afraid that to push for women's voting rights would cost the movement some valuable support, but Stanton insisted that this resolution remain a part of the convention. During the conference, every resolution passed without a hitch; but the women's voting resolution, which had the support of Frederick Douglass, only passed by a narrow margin. Disregarding the jeers of male opponents in the audience, the delegates issued a Declaration of Sentiments and Resolutions, a document that was based to a great extent on the Declaration of Independence. The convention's declaration proposed an eleven-point plan for helping women achieve equality with men.

After the convention, Gilbert read Sojourner an article in Douglass's newspaper, the *North Star,* that summarized the convention. Douglass believed, "We are free to say that in respect to political rights, we hold woman to be justly entitled to all we claim for man."

Sojourner listened to these articles and conversations around her. While it was true that in the nineteenth century, white women had few political rights, black free women had even fewer rights. A slave woman had *no* rights. She was not only brutally mistreated by white men and women, but often the black men would also abuse her, modeling their actions after their white masters.

One of the outspoken women authors during Sojourner's lifetime was Lydia Marie Child. Known as a humanist, Child believed in the dignity of every human being. In her writings, Child described the social status of the black slave woman, saying, "She is unprotected by either law or public opinion. She is the property of her master, and her daughters are his property. . . . They must be entirely subservient to the will of their owner on pain of being whipped as near to death as will comport with his interest or quite to death if it suits his pleasure."

White women were in a larger cage than slave women. They were controlled by the men in their lives—fathers, brothers, and uncles—who trained them to believe they were too "fragile" to make social or political decisions. During one of his visits from England to America, author Charles Dickens observed that "American men accorded their women more deference, lavished more money on them, regarded them with more respect than was accorded the women of any country. But they didn't particularly like them."

Although white women had some rights, they couldn't serve on juries, hold public office, or even manage their own finances (if they had any money to manage). In the case of a divorce, the husband was automatically given custody of the children because, as one judge said, "If she had been a good wife and mother, sharp on her duties, then her husband wouldn't be seeking separation."

Women would never be able to change these practices in the United States without the legal power to vote for elected officials. With the status quo, they remained powerless.

As Sojourner listened and saw the struggle of all women for freedom, she decided that women's rights was a cause worth fighting for.

After Olive Gilbert read Frederick Douglass's autobiography to Sojourner, she encouraged her to write her own story. "I'll write it for you," Gilbert volunteered. "You dictate it to me."

Garrison encouraged the publication of Sojourner's story because he saw it would add to the growing number of anti-slavery stories. Her story would reveal how slaves in the North were treated. He offered to print the book and even wrote the introduction to *The Narrative of Sojourner Truth: A Northern Slave.*

The book was printed in 1850, the same year that Congress passed a more rigid version of the Fugitive Slave Act as part of the Compromise of 1850. After the Mexican War, Representative David Wilmot of Pennsylvania introduced an amendment to a bill in Congress that prohibited slavery in any territory acquired as a result of the Mexican War or the Southwest Territory. The House passed this amendment, but the Senate defeated it. Bitter debates followed the vote, and fistfights broke out on the Senate floor. The debate was over the fate of two possible new states—California and New Mexico (New Mexico, then including present-day Arizona, southern Colorado, southern Utah, and southern Nevada, was designated a territory but denied statehood). If even one state was admitted to the United States as a free state, the balance of power between Northern and Southern senators would be upset. At that time, the power was evenly divided at fifteen Southern states and fifteen Northern states.

In September 1850, Congress passed the famous compromise. The second largest state in terms of total area, California was admitted to the Union as a free state in exchange for a law to replace the poorly enforced Fugitive Slave Law of 1793. The new Fugitive Slave Act of 1850 required Northern states to return runaway slaves to their masters.

But this compromise settled nothing. The Southerners continued to hide behind states' rights to protect slavery, and the abolitionists of the North were more determined than ever to fight slavery in the West. Many people echoed the feelings of poet Ralph Waldo Emerson, who said, "This filthy enactment. . .I will not obey it, by God."

Angry and upset by the new Fugitive Slave Act, anti-slavery sympathizers expanded the Underground Railroad network, which each year helped more than a thousand slaves to escape from the South. In some communities in the North, slave catchers began to meet armed resistance when they confronted runaway slaves and their supporters.

Not every Northerner supported the anti-slavery people. Many people in the North maintained that the Fugitive Slave Act had to be obeyed so peace could be maintained between the North and the South. These people accused the abolitionists of trying to divide the nation. They hated the blacks and wanted all freed slaves to be returned to the South or shipped to Africa.

The next month, October, Sojourner traveled to Worcester, Massachusetts, to speak at that year's national women's rights convention. There she listened—along with a thousand others—to such distinguished speakers as Stanton, Mott, Stone, Douglass, and Garrison.

Most of the clergy took an active role in resisting the women's meeting. One minister promised to expel women in his church who attended the meeting, while another clergyman told his church that these meetings were "sponsored by the devil."

The male-dominated press that reported on the convention called the conference a hen party and chided the women, saying they were "fe-he-males" or "hens that wanted to crow."

Yet on that day in late October 1850, over a thousand people from eleven states participated in the conference. Several men such as Douglass, Garrison, Pillsbury, and Phillips had come to the conference to throw their support to the women's cause. As Sojourner looked around the audience, she noticed that she was the only black woman.

A self-educated physician, Helen Hunt officially opened the meeting by reading a statement from Elizabeth Cady Stanton. Stanton regretted that she could not attend the conference because she was at home awaiting the birth of her fourth child. Then the chairwoman of the conference gave a powerful speech that concluded, "We claim for women all blessings which the other sex has, solely, or by her aid, achieved for itself."

It took all of the patience that Sojourner could muster to listen to the various speakers. Some of them discussed whether women should be able to keep their jewelry after a divorce or whether women were more liberated by wearing bloomers, a pant-type dress, which had supposedly freed the body and allowed more physical exercise. To Sojourner's way of thinking, these issues were irrelevant. The whole idea of bloomers amused her. Many a day, Sojourner had worn pantlike dresses as she had worked over a washtub. The style held no glamour or attraction in her eyes. She was more concerned about whether a divorced mother should be allowed to keep her children.

Then Lucretia Mott, a young schoolteacher, addressed the conference. She spoke passionately about being paid less than a male teacher only because she was a woman. Lucy Stone, a graduate from Oberlin College, spoke and was equally concerned with this issue of equal pay for equal work. Stone told about refusing to use her husband's last name so she could show people that he was not her "master." Self-worth and equal pay for equal work were issues that Sojourner could understand and identify with. Her interest in the speeches increased. As different people spoke, she made mental notes about issues that she would like to address.

Toward the conclusion of the conference, Sojourner was asked to speak to the convention. She began, "Sisters, I am not clear on what you be after. If women want any rights more than they've got, why don't they just take them and not be talking about it?"

While the goals for the conference may have been fuzzy at first, by the conclusion of the convention, the women had clarified their goals. Their motto clearly stated their primary objective, "Equality before the law without distinction of sex or color." Sojourner left the conference feeling inspired and motivated. From that time on, she included equality for women in her speeches.

However, the problem of attaining equal rights for women was more complex than Sojourner was willing to admit to the convention. A sizable number of men strongly opposed equality for women and were ready to fight in order to preserve the status quo. Those who pushed for women's rights often disagreed among themselves about the best way to achieve their goals. Some women wanted to gain their rights in the courts of law, while others believed that putting pressure on political parties and congressmen would achieve better results. For years, the debates continued at annual conventions that were held throughout the United States.

Yet Sojourner's defiant message at the 1850 women's rights convention stirred the ranks of the nation's feminists and abolitionists, as well as any oppressed person who wanted equality. "Why not just take your rights?" Sojourner had asked. Many Americans who had been deprived of their rights were beginning to ask the same question.

SEVEN

After Sojourner Truth published her autobiography in 1850, she became well-known to both the anti-slavery and the women's rights movements. William Lloyd Garrison and his associate Wendell Phillips convinced Sojourner to lend her splendid speaking voice to the abolitionist cause. Soon she was traveling with other lecturers throughout New England. While traveling on the lecture circuit, Sojourner sold many copies of her book, and with the proceeds continued to pay on her home in Northampton.

By the time Sojourner joined the lecture circuit, she looked much older than her fifty-three years. Her black hair had turned gray, her forehead had become deeply lined with wrinkles, and she wore metal-rimmed glasses to help her fading eyesight. For almost every occasion, Sojourner wore a plain black dress and a long white shawl. A white handkerchief wrapped around her head formed a turban. From her appearance, some people guessed that she was in her nineties.

As a result, the crowds at the abolitionist meetings were astonished at the vigor with which Sojourner Truth attacked the institution of slavery. In her lectures, she denounced slave owners as sinners who would someday soon feel God's wrath. Most of these audiences were filled with white people—mostly men—and few of them had ever heard a black speaker other than Frederick Douglass give a public address. They found it interesting that a black woman would publicly state her views on slavery.

Not only was Sojourner smart, but she also knew how to control hecklers. Once a man shouted, "What you have to say is no more important than a flea."

"Well," she answered, "then I hope to keep you scratchin'!"

Audiences were surprised at Sojourner's speaking style. Most speakers tried to pronounce their words beautifully and often used formal and flowery speech, but Sojourner didn't try to imitate that style. Instead, she cast a spell over her listeners with the rough, uneducated manner and language of an unschooled slave girl who had never learned to read or write. Unlike some speakers who droned on for hours, she impressed her listeners with her ability to cut to the heart of a complex issue in just a few words.

Frederick Douglass described Sojourner Truth as

"that strange compound of wit and wisdom, of wild enthusiasm, and flintlike common sense, who seemed to feel it her duty to trip me up in my speeches and to ridicule my efforts to speak and act like a person of cultivation and refinement."

Soon Sojourner became known for her simple but moving anti-slavery speeches and her witty, biting attacks on people who continued to own slaves yet said they were Christians. She knew that many Northerners wanted to pretend that slavery was strictly a problem in the South. To these people, millions of black slaves were practically invisible. Sojourner believed it was her mission to force all Americans to confront the nationwide moral problem of slavery.

Throughout the nation, people were divided on the issue of slavery. Whether in the North or South, opinions varied. Sometimes people were hostile to Sojourner's messages. Some of them threatened her life with angry mobs. During such occasions, she mustered all her courage, stood her ground, and continued speaking. She was surprised at the angry reactions. They had forgotten that the United States had been founded by people who were themselves fleeing the tyranny of others.

As the abolitionists continued their work to end slavery, some slaves also worked to free themselves. One of the main characters in the struggle for freedom was Harriet Tubman, a fugitive slave and a conductor on the Underground Railroad.

It wasn't until many years later that Sojourner Truth

met Tubman, but she had heard about her work and admired the woman's bold spirit and determination. In 1849, Tubman had escaped from slavery, but she returned to the South so she could lead others to freedom. Because of her work on the Underground Railroad, Harriet had a price on her head, but that didn't matter to her. She eventually made twenty trips back to the South and led hundreds of slaves to freedom.

Anti-slavery speakers delighted to tell stories about Harriet Tubman and other daring escapees. One of the most thrilling escapes they told was the story of William and Ellen Craft. In 1848, Ellen, a fair-skinned black, disguised herself as a white man who was traveling with his slave—in fact, her husband. Using this disguise, the Crafts escaped from Georgia and made a mockery of a social system based on color inferiority. Why, the white people couldn't even tell who was one of their own race!

Sojourner watched events like the Crafts' escape unfold around her, and often she expressed joy at being near people who were so passionate about freedom from slavery. Since she hadn't been able to sell many copies of her autobiography because she didn't have the national recognition that Douglass and some other abolitionists had, she would attend the abolitionist gatherings and sell her book after the conclusion of the meeting.

One evening, during a meeting in the late 1850s, Garrison saw his friend Sojourner in the audience and said with a matter-of-fact tone, "Sojourner will say a few words, after which Wendell Phillips will follow."

Sojourner hadn't come to the meeting prepared to speak, but she couldn't pass up the opportunity. When she stood, her tall presence commanded attention. Then, as she had done at the camp meetings, Sojourner used the strength of her voice to capture the attention of her audience. She began by singing one of her original hymns:

"I am pleading for my people,
A poor downtrodden race,
Who dwell in freedom's boasted land
With no abiding place.

"I am pleading that my people
May have their rights restored;
For they have long been toiling,
And yet have no reward.

"They are forced the crops to culture,
But not for them they yield,
Although both late and early
They labor in the field.

"Whilst I bear upon my body
The scars of many a gash,
I am pleading for my people
Who groan beneath the lash."

Then, without any fanfare, Truth began her speech,

making each point simply yet eloquently. "Well, children," she began, "I was born a slave in Ulster County, New York. I don't know if it was summer or winter, fall or spring. I don't even know what day of the week it was. They don't care when a slave is born or when he dies. . . just how much work they can do."

After telling the tragic story of her father's death and her struggle to get her son, Peter, back, she closed her message saying, "God will not make His face shine upon a nation that holds with slavery." The crowd applauded and cheered. Some of the people cried while others sat stunned and silent. It was a hard act for even Wendell Phillips to follow.

That evening, Sojourner sold twice as many books as before. She decided to go on a speaking tour. . .to sell books and to spread the "truth" as she understood it. After people had asked about her hymns, she made some of them into a booklet and sold them along with her biography. After each evening of selling books, Sojourner dutifully put aside some of the money to pay for the printing of her book and some to pay Sam Hill for building her home.

For a while, Sojourner traveled and spoke with Garrison and George Thompson, an English abolitionist. Often they reached places where their figures had been burned in effigy. Sojourner's messages always managed to stir the emotions of a sympathetic gathering or inflame the tempers of a hostile group. No one could be passive when listening to Sojourner Truth.

Sometimes Sojourner had confrontations with individual preachers. Once a young revivalist called on her, begging her to be reconciled to God. Sojourner replied, "Reconciled to God! Why, I ain't got nothing against God! Why should I be reconciled to Him for? God's always been mighty good to me; He called me out of slavery and has taken good care of me ever since. You ministers would have kept me in bondage. Why, I haven't got anything against Him."

At another anti-slavery meeting, when abolitionists were attacking the church for its reluctance to fight slavery, a clergyman said that he was afraid God might knock him down at any moment for listening to such blasphemy. According to a friend, Sojourner told that clergyman, "Don't be scared. I don't expect God has ever heard of you!"

And at a different anti-slavery meeting, an orthodox clergyman who was visiting the meeting protested that the anti-slavery speakers were "women and donkeys." Sojourner replied that in a Bible story another minister, Balaam, also got "mighty mad" at a donkey, the one he was riding on, because it carried him off the road. But the reason the donkey went off the road was that God had sent an angel to direct them not to go any farther. Only the donkey, not the minister, was able to understand what the angel was directing them to do.

In spite of these confrontations, Sojourner found it natural to associate with ministers. Several clergyman wrote sympathetic articles about her in the newspapers.

Despite her outward appearance of simplicity, she understood how churches could help pull people along toward what she considered to be the necessary remaking of both individuals and society. Once in a discussion among Progressive Friends, the radical abolitionist Henry C. Wright insisted on attacking churches bitterly for their cooperation with slavery. Wright urged that these places be named "so-called" churches. Sojourner disagreed with Wright. "We ought to be like Christ," she argued. "He said, 'Father, forgive them; for they know not what they do.' If we want to lead the people, we must not be out of their sight." Sojourner believed in approaching the public with a hopeful attitude and in using widely acceptable, noncontroversial Christian teaching in her public appeals.

At one meeting in Syracuse in 1850, the crowd had come to hear George Thompson speak and were angered when Sojourner came to the podium first. She quieted the crowd by saying, "I'll tell you what Thompson is going to say to you. He is going to argue that the poor Negroes ought to be out of slavery and in the heavenly state of freedom. But, children, I'm against slavery because I want to keep the white folks who hold slaves from getting sent to hell." Sojourner's basic concerns undoubtedly involved her fellow blacks, but she was so perceptive that she spoke directly to the needs of her white audience. The meeting was saved, and the crowd listened with interest to Sojourner and then to Thompson.

Early in 1851, Garrison planned an anti-slavery speaking trip with Thompson. He invited Sojourner to accompany them and explained that the meetings would give her a chance to sell her books. Many years later, Sojourner recalled for Garrison the meaning of those days of travel. "My heart is glowing with the remembrance of George Thompson's kindness to me. I had been publishing my *Narrative* and owed for the entire edition. It was a great debt for me, and every cent that I could obtain went to pay for it. You [Garrison] said to me, 'I am going on a lecture tour. Come with us and you will have a good chance to dispose of your book.' You generously offered to bear my expenses, and it was arranged that I should meet you in Springfield.

"On the appointed day, I was there, but you were not at the hotel. I inquired for Mr. Thompson and was shown into his room. He received me and seated me with as much courtesy and cordiality as if I had been the highest lady in the land. Then he informed me that you were too ill to leave home, but if I would go with himself and Mr. G. W. Putman, it would be all the same. 'But,' I said, 'I have no money,' and Mr. Garrison offered to pay my passage.

"He said, 'I'll bear your expenses, Sojourner. Come with us!' And so I went.

"Mr. Thompson accompanied me to the cars and carried my bag. At the hotel tables, he seated me beside himself and never seemed to know that I was poor and a black woman. At the meetings, he recommended my books saying, 'Sojourner Truth has a narrative of her life. It is very interesting. Buy largely, friends!' Good man! Genuine gentleman! God bless George Thompson, the great-hearted friend of my race!"

During February and March of 1851, Sojourner traveled with Thompson, Putman, and others as they made their way by train from Springfield, Massachusetts, west into New York State. They spoke at a series of anti-slavery conventions. Sometimes they were joined by Frederick Douglass. At each meeting, Sojourner sold her books.

Thompson, Sojourner, and others traveled throughout western New York during 1851, speaking to various kinds of audiences. Many of these were unruly mobs whose primary purpose was to disrupt the meetings or fluster or injure the speakers. At all times, Sojourner maintained her dignity and never showed any fear before the greater strength and numbers of her opponents.

At Union Village, New York, Sojourner made a speech that was reported to be "in her peculiar manner." She said that "while others had been talking about the poor slave. . .I am going to talk about the poor slave-holder. What will happen to him? I'm afraid that he is going to hell unless he changes." Putnam wrote about the meeting in Garrison's *Liberator* and said that "Truth was most kindly received by the audience, who pressed around her to purchase her books, and who saw in her proof of the natural equality to say the leave of the Negro and the white. It is devoutly to be wished that all whites were her equals."

By the time the traveling speakers reached Rochester, New York, where they ended their trip, Putnam had become enthusiastic about Sojourner. Though she could neither read nor write, he reported, "She will often speak with an ability [that] surprises the educated and refined. She possesses a mind of rare power, and often, in the course of her short speeches, will throw out gems of thought. But the truly Christian spirit [that] pervades all she says endears her to all who know her. Though she has suffered all the ills of slavery, she forgives all who have wronged her most freely. She said her home should be open to the man who had held her as a slave and who had so much wronged her. She would feed him and take care of him if he was hungry and poor. 'Oh, friends,' she said, 'pity the poor slaveholder, and pray for him. It troubles me more than anything else, what will become of the poor slaveholder, in all his guilt and all his impenitence. God will take care of the poor trampled slave, but where will the slaveholder be when eternity begins?'"

In mid-1853, after a successful tour through the Midwest and a fall filled with travel and speeches, Sojourner Truth was tired of traveling and decided to take a period for rest. That winter, she stayed with Isaac and Amy Post, well-known Quaker abolitionists in Rochester, New York. At the Posts' home, letters from her children finally caught up with her. The letters made Sojourner want to see them even more. Diana wrote about how Dumont had "gone west" with some of his sons, but that before leaving he had become a strong abolitionist and told them, "slavery was an evil institution." The change didn't surprise Sojourner because the last time she had seen her old master, his attitude had been changing.

In an updated version of her autobiography, Sojourner recalled her old master John Dumont's words: "Now the sin of slavery is clearly written out, and so much talked against—why, the whole world cries out against it!— that if anyone says he don't know, and has not heard, he must, I think, be a liar. In my slaveholding days, there were few that spoke against it, and these few made little impression on anyone. Had it been as it is now, think you I could have held slaves? No! I should not have dared to do it, but should have emancipated every one of them." These powerful words came from the same man Sojourner had fled in order to gain her freedom. Dumont had completely changed his attitude.

After reading these letters from her children, Sojourner made a trip to visit them. Her daughters were living in New York and New England; some had married and had children. Truth's oldest grandchild, Hannah's son, James Caldwell, was already nine years old. After enjoying a pleasant stay with her daughters' families, Sojourner set out for her house in Northampton, with a brief stopover in Andover, Massachusetts, the home of abolitionist writer Harriet Beecher Stowe.

Harriet, the daughter of Lyman Beecher and the wife of Calvin Ellis Stowe (both Calvinist clergymen and abolitionists) had written the novel *Uncle Tom's Cabin* in

1852 in response to the Fugitive Slave Act, and it had received great international attention. One reviewer said about the book that it "penetrated the walls of Congress and made the politicians tremble. It startled statesmen, who scented danger near." Stowe's novel aroused a great deal of anger among Southerners, who accused her of greatly exaggerating the sufferings endured among slaves. Abolitionists praised her for presenting a true picture of the injustices of the slave system. Her book helped to fan the anti-slavery fires in the North.

As soon as a copy of this book was available to her, Sojourner had it read to her. The story is about Tom, a slave who saves his master's daughter and is promised his freedom. But the master dies before Tom is actually freed. The family falls on hard times, and Tom is sold to a horrible slave owner named Simon Legree. Legree tries everything to degrade Tom, but Tom holds firmly to his religious convictions. In a frenzy of anger, Legree beats Tom to death.

Sojourner's meeting with Stowe was a memorable occasion for both the small white novelist and the tall black preacher. They immediately liked each other and respected the work that each was doing to end slavery. One evening, Sojourner spoke to a gathering at Mrs. Stowe's home. Later, Stowe wrote about the meetings, saying, "I do not recollect ever to have been conversant with anyone who had more of that silent subtle power which we call personal presence than this woman. No princess could have received a drawing room with more composed dignity than Sojourner her audience. She stood among them, calm, erect, as one of her own native palm trees waving alone in the desert."

Recalling her guest's poise in that white, middle-class household of educated men and women, professors and preachers of renown, Stowe painted this picture of Sojourner: "She seemed perfectly self-possessed and at ease; in fact, there was an almost unconscious superiority, not unmixed with a solemn twinkle of humor, in the odd, composed manner in which she looked down at me. Her whole air had at times a gloomy sort of drollery which impressed one strangely."

Regretting the human loss that occurred when some people enslaved other human beings, Stowe wrote, "I can not but think that Sojourner with the same culture might have spoken as eloquent and undying as the African St. Augustine or Tertullian. How grand and queenly a woman she might have been, with her wonderful physical vigor, her great heaving seas of emotion, her power of spiritual conception, her quick penetration, and her boundless energy!"

After returning home, Sojourner decided to continue her speaking tours. At each of the abolitionist meetings she attended, she always brought along several copies of her autobiography to sell as well as a new item: postcards that bore her photograph and the legend, "I Sell the Shadow to Support the Substance." She called these cards her *cartes de viste,* which is French for "calling cards." She also brought her "Book of Life," an album in which she collected short notes and autographs from many people she had met through her travels.

By the mid-1850s, Sojourner Truth had become known throughout much of the United States. However, she wasn't the only black woman whose anti-slavery efforts drew attention. During this period, Harriet Tubman, the poet Frances E. W. Harper, and the abolitionist Sarah Remond often addressed women's anti-slavery conventions and women's rights meetings as well.

As Sojourner continued to speak out in favor of the end of slavery, she insisted that freedom for blacks must be accompanied by freedom for women. "If colored men get their rights and not colored women," she explained to the audience of a women's rights conference, "colored men will be masters over the women, and it will be just as bad as before."

At a women's rights convention in New York, a group of especially hostile men jeered Sojourner whenever she spoke. She told them that she knew how much it annoyed them to have a black woman speak about justice and freedom. "Blacks and women," she said, "have all been thrown down so low that nobody thought we'd ever get up again. . .but we will come up again, and now here I am."

This kind of uncompromising attitude eventually enabled Sojourner and other feminists to bring about some reforms for women. In New York, Susan B. Anthony collected ten thousand signatures for a petition requesting that married women be allowed to control their own property. The state legislature ultimately approved Anthony's petition and also gave divorced women the right to share custody of their children.

Throughout this period, Sojourner continued to travel and speak at different conventions. She felt that God was telling her to go west, and as always, she obeyed. She went to Ohio, which was a free state and one of the main arteries on the Underground Railroad. Despite the strong anti-slavery movement in Ohio, there were also a lot of pro-slavery feelings, especially in the rural areas.

Audience reaction to Sojourner varied greatly. Sometimes she was well-received, but more often than not, she ended up hoarse from yelling her speech over the jeers and hoots from protesters. One day, she was met outside a city by an angry mob. They told her in clear terms, "Go somewhere else." She walked away from the mob but circled around the town and came in from another direction. On another occasion, a sheriff came to arrest Sojourner and her companion to protect their lives from the angry crowd. For her to give up was out of the question, despite the growing danger.

While lecturing in Ohio, Sojourner learned about a woman's rights convention in Akron, Ohio, which was organized by Mrs. Frances Gage. Truth decided to attend.

Hundreds of women and men gathered at a local church so they could hear various speakers. Clearly, the audience had mixed opinions about this topic of women's rights. Most of the men had come with firm prejudices against the movement. Many of the men were ministers committed to discrediting the movement as anti-Christian. A few women attended with their husbands, who supported the women's rights position. Finally, the seasoned feminists were also in attendance, because their goals and aspirations were being addressed.

For the most part, the gathering of these different viewpoints was congenial. Suddenly the doors to the church swung open, and a tall, proud figure stood framed in the doorway. "It's Sojourner Truth," someone whispered. Slowly Sojourner walked to the front of the auditorium. She soon noticed that she was the only black person in the room. Since every seat was filled, she took a seat on the steps leading to the pulpit. As she sat, Sojourner folded her arms and listened.

Soon the people in the room were buzzing with excitement. Would this black woman be permitted to speak to the convention?

The convention listened to speaker after speaker. Each one tried to impress the crowd with his or her opinion. Several ministers tried to disrupt the meeting by encouraging women who "feared God" to immediately leave. When this technique didn't succeed, the clergymen used the same worn-out logic that mankind had used for centuries to oppress women and blacks—God created women to be weak and blacks to be a subservient race.

One minister argued that Jesus Christ was a man and that if God had intended for women to be equal God "would have at that time made some gesture to show His intent."

Another speaker quoted a newspaper article that suggested that "a woman's place is at home taking care of her children." Sojourner listened to this argument and thought, *What? Nobody ever gave me that opportunity!*

Still another minister stood and made the persistent argument that woman had sinned first and was therefore inferior to man.

At a brief intermission, a group of women cornered the moderator of the convention, Frances Gage. "Will Sojourner Truth be allowed to speak?" they asked. Some of these women were afraid that if this black woman spoke, it would confuse the issue and even discredit their cause. After all, they reasoned, What has women's rights to do with abolitionism? Some of the leaders threatened that they would leave if Sojourner addressed the convention.

"Let's just see," Mrs. Gage answered without making a commitment in either direction.

The entire first day, Sojourner simply listened. Then during the second day, she turned to the chairwoman and asked for permission to speak. For a moment, Frances Gage hesitated; then she simply introduced the black woman as "Sojourner Truth." No other introduction was required.

Sojourner had garnered a great deal of experience speaking to hostile crowds. As she looked around the room, she could see the anger and resentment on the faces of some of the people. Fearlessly but gently, Sojourner took control of the situation. First, as she stood at the podium, she removed her sunbonnet, folded it neatly, and set it aside. These slow and deliberate actions had a calming effect on the crowd.

Throughout the day before and that morning, Sojourner had heard preachers—men who were supposed to know better—use the Bible to support their own purposes. She had heard enough of such talk and had grown angry and ready to do battle using God's own truth. With no prepared speech, Sojourner began to speak in her deep, husky voice.

"Well, children, where there is so much racket, there must be somethin' out of kilter. . . . The white men will be in a fix pretty soon. But what's all this about anyway?

"That man over there. . . ," Sojourner said as she pointed to a minister who had said a woman's place was to be a mother, wife and companion, good sister, and loving niece. "He says women need to be helped into carriages and lifted over ditches and to have the best everywhere. Nobody ever helps me into carriages, over mud puddles, or gets me any best places."

The black woman pulled her frame to her entire height and looked out over the crowd with a defiant gesture and said, "And ain't I a woman?"

Then she turned to face the men who were sitting on the platform behind her. She said, "Look at me!" Then she pulled back her sleeve and showed her right arm and raised it into the air. As though with a single voice, the audience gasped. Her dark arm was muscular and made strong from years of hard work. "I have plowed, and I have planted." She was recalling her years as a slave on the Dumont estate, where she had worked for her freedom. "And I have gathered the crops into the barns. And no man could work stronger than me." She paused and once again asked the audience, "And ain't I a woman?

"I have borne twelve children and watched them be sold into slavery, and when I cried out in a mother's grief, no one heard me but Jesus. And ain't I a woman?" Without a doubt Sojourner was referring to her mother, Mau Mau, because Sojourner had only had five children.

Then point by point, Sojourner took on the religious speakers. "You say Jesus was a man, so that means God favors men over women. Where did your Christ come from?" She asked again, "Where did He come from?" Then she answered her own question. "From God and a woman. Man had nothing to do with Him."

Sojourner challenged the widely held belief that women were less intelligent than men and blacks had no intellect at all. "Suppose a man's mind holds a quart, and a woman's mind doesn't hold more than a pint; if her pint is full, it's as good as a quart." With straightforward common sense, Sojourner ripped at the heart of the various arguments.

She then directed her comments to the women in the audience. "If the first woman God ever made was strong enough to turn the world upside down all alone, these women together ought to be able to turn it back and get it right side up again, and now that they are asking to do it, the men better let 'em."

Few of the listeners could understand the full

meaning of Sojourner's hard-hitting speech. It was doubt-ful that the rural Ohio community was ready to accept the claim that took women's rights across the boundaries of race, class, and the bondage of slavery.

Sojourner proclaimed the truth in simple terms. For people who had good reason, racism and sexism were unacceptable.

EIGHT

Sojourner left the Akron conference with a new banner that a friend of hers had made. It stated, "Proclaim liberty throughout all the land unto all the inhabitants thereof." She loaded up with six hundred copies of her book and traveled around Indiana and Ohio in a borrowed horse and buggy. Sojourner made speeches against slavery and in support of the women's rights movement. She never planned her route or worried about food, clothing, or shelter. Often she permitted her horse to choose the direction that she would travel. "The Lord will guide and protect me," she insisted.

The Fugitive Slave Act continued to stir controversy. During an anniversary convention of the Anti-Slavery Society in Salem, Ohio, Frederick Douglass told the audience that he believed a war was the only lasting means for freedom. This stance was a marked change from his previous nonviolent position and strained his relationship with Garrison. "Nevertheless," Douglass said, "there is no longer any hope for justice other than bloody rebellion. Slavery must end in blood."

Sojourner was in the audience, and his words struck her heart. *There is no hope. . . . There is no hope!* she thought. Leaping to her feet, she called out to her old friend in a voice that trembled with emotion, "Frederick, is God dead?"

Douglass understood what his old friend meant—she was asking if he had completely lost his faith. "No," Douglass answered quickly, "and because God is not dead, slavery can only end in blood."

Sojourner disagreed with this outlook on slavery. She was convinced that slavery could end without violence.

From her travels and speeches, Sojourner Truth's fame and stature grew as an abolitionist and feminist who had wit and wisdom. As the word spread across the Midwestern countryside, even her opponents respected her.

Once a heckler in an Ohio town shouted that the Constitution didn't say a word against slavery. "Are you against the Constitution, old woman?"

"Well, children," Sojourner started in her usual manner, "I talks to God and God talks to me. This morning I was walking out and I climbed over a fence. I saw the wheat holding up its head, looking so big. I goes up and takes hold of it. Would you believe it, there was no wheat there! I says, 'God, what's the matter with this wheat?' And He says to me, 'Sojourner, there's a little weevil in it.'"

"What's that got to do with the Constitution?" the heckler yelled at Sojourner.

With a firm wave of her hand, she told the audience that she wasn't finished with the thought about the Constitution. "I hears talk about the Constitution and the rights of man. I comes up and I takes hold of this Constitution. It looks mighty big. And I feels for my rights. But they are not there. Then I ask, 'God, what ails this Constitution?' And you know what He says to me? God says, 'Sojourner, there's a little weevil in it.'" Ohio farmers in that 1852 audience could understand this story all too well. Their wheat crop had been ruined by the tiny beetle known as a weevil.

Later that fall, Sojourner spoke at the anti-slavery meeting in Ashtabula County, Ohio, along with her good friend, Parker Pillsbury. In fact, Pillsbury was the primary speaker at the conference and gave an eloquent and moving speech against slavery. He was followed by a young lawyer who spoke for almost an hour about the inferiority of blacks. This speaker said that blacks were "fit only for slavery. As a race, the Negro is only a connecting link between man and animals." As a thunderstorm broke loudly outside, the man went on to say that God was punishing Pillsbury and his colleagues for the things against God that Pillsbury had said.

The lawyer called out that the storm was God's wrath, come to show that He was angry with the anti-slavery movement. As the man continued speaking, Sojourner suddenly stepped out of the darkness. Dressed in her familiar gray dress, shawl, and white turban, she approached the stage. She looked like an avenger and doubtless was more fearful looking than any thunderstorm.

"Are you afraid the Lord has sent the storm in wrath at our opinions?" she asked the lawyer, while leaning over as if to comfort a little boy. "Child," she said, "don't be scared."

Then she continued in her calm, deep voice, "When I was a slave away down there in New York, and there was some particularly bad work to be done, some colored woman was sure to be called on to do it. And when I heard that man talking away there as he did for almost a whole hour, I said to myself, 'Here's one spot of work sure that's fit for colored folks to clean up after.'" Truth reminded her listeners that she was proud of being pure African American, without a single drop of white blood in her veins. She told the young man, "Child, you are not going to be harmed. I don't expect God's ever heard tell of you."

Not every audience that Sojourner faced was friendly, but over and over she proved how her quick wit could quiet any disruptions from a hostile crowd. In 1853, she attended the women's rights convention held at the Broadway Tabernacle in New York. The hall was packed with hecklers and opponents to women's rights. Chroniclers of the movement called this meeting "the Mob Convention." When Sojourner stood to speak, the crowd roared in reaction to her skin color.

She began her remarks by referring to the noisy audience as people with either the spirit of geese or of snakes.

She proceeded to speak above the roar and finally managed to quiet the crowd. "I know that it feels a-kind of hissing- and tickling-like to see a colored woman get up and tell you about things and women's rights," she said. "We have all been thrown down so low that nobody thought we'd ever get up again, but we have been long enough trodden now; we will come up again, and now here I am."

Then Sojourner talked about Queen Esther and King Ahasuerus, a story from the Bible in which a woman came forward to set things right—just as women in the nineteenth century were doing. Sojourner told her audience, "When she comes to demand them, don't you hear how sons hiss at their mothers like snakes, because they ask for their rights; and can they ask for anything less? . . . But we'll have our rights; see if we don't. You can't stop us from them; see if you can. You may hiss as much as you like, but it is coming. Women don't get half as much rights as they ought to; we want more, and we will have it." Sojourner then chided her enemies in the crowd for "hissing like snakes and geese," and she reminded them that Jesus required them to honor both father and mother. The crowd responded to her speech with loud applause. It was a huge success.

Throughout the Midwest, Sojourner continued to travel and speak against slavery. At times she felt pressed to defend her stance against the onslaught of criticism hurled at blacks from Northern "meddlers." Many of these opponents quoted George Fitzhugh, a

Virginia slaveholder, who wrote in 1854 that blacks were better off as slaves in America than in "a far more cruel slavery in Africa, or from idolatry and cannibalism, and every brutal vice and crime that can disgrace humanity."

Sojourner was quick to respond to those who used Fitzhugh's error-filled material. "Be careful," she'd say forcefully. "God will not stand with wrong; never mind how right you think you be."

Sojourner never permitted herself to be intimidated or put down but rose to every occasion and gracefully withdrew if she felt it was wise. Time and time again, she showed her courage as she traveled through New Jersey, New York, Ohio, Indiana, Michigan, and many other states.

As she addressed her audiences, Sojourner blended tones of pride and modesty. She addressed her audience as "children" and individuals as "honey," showing affection for all sympathizers, and it endeared her to many people. The salty wit, characteristic of her speaking, appeared on many occasions. She was full of amusing sayings, some of which have survived and been used by other speakers. On one occasion, she began her talk by saying, "Children, I've come here like the rest of you to hear what I have to say," an opening line that a distinguished lecturer borrowed many years later. Sometimes she coined new expressions. Instead of saying that every person had to stand on his or her own two feet, Sojourner said, "Every tub has to stand on its own bottom."

Not only did her humor and sharpness make

Sojourner an effective speaker against slavery, but her experience of having felt the whip's lash influenced her delivery. She explained, "As now, when I hear them tell of whipping women on the bare flesh, it makes my flesh crawl, and my very hair rise on my head." But more than this, she had the ability to appeal to white people by shaming them or encouraging them—or even complimenting them.

While Frederick Douglass or Harriet Tubman did a vital job of speaking to black people, Sojourner took a different role. She was one of the few black people who spoke almost exclusively to white people, individually or in groups, and few blacks worked as closely as she did with the white abolitionists. A number of stories demonstrate her talent for subduing racist mobs and destroying racists arguments. She could deal with white people from all persuasions.

One of her favorite memories was about "finding Jesus." She spoke of a questioning voice within her that wondered at her love for all creatures. " 'There's the white folks that have abused you, and beat you, and abused your people—think of them.' But then there came another rush of love through my soul, and I cried out loud—'Lord, Lord, I can love even the white folks!' " And indeed Sojourner could confront the white people without bitterness, fear, or timidity.

The country was divided North against South. But people wondered about the territories in the West. Many thought that the expansion of slavery into the western sections of the United States had been regulated through the Missouri Compromise of 1820. At that time, Missouri had been admitted into the United States as a slave state while Maine had been admitted as a free state. Because the seats in the Senate remained balanced, it was acceptable to both sides that slavery would be outlawed in the lands from the Louisiana Purchase north of the 36 degrees 30 minutes parallel.

But the tension between North and South continued to grow, and everyone knew that something had to be done. Senator Stephen A. Douglas from Illinois introduced the Kansas–Nebraska Bill, which was passed in May 1854. The bill gave the citizens in a territory that wanted to become a state the right to choose whether they wanted to be a free state or a slave state. Unfortunately, the bill didn't accomplish what its creators hoped. Instead, the Kansas Territory, located west of Missouri, became a political hotbed.

Mobs of ruffians from Missouri crossed over into Kansas to vote for Kansas to be admitted as a slave state. Free-Soil Kansas residents rejected the vote and refused to accept the provisional slave-state government. Armed conflict threatened to break out.

In May 1856, pro-slavery forces attacked Lawrence, Kansas, which was a Free-Soil settlement. A radical abolitionist named John Brown had gone to Kansas to push for its entrance into the United States as a free state. After the destruction of Lawrence, Brown led a counterattack against a pro-slavery settlement in Pottawatomie

Creek. Five people were killed, and the incident became so heated that Preston S. Brooks, a congressman from South Carolina, physically attacked Massachusetts Senator Charles Sumner on the Senate floor after Sumner made an anti-slavery speech. Sumner was so badly beaten that he remained an invalid for more than three years.

Brooks gave Sojourner and other anti-slavery speakers plenty of ammunition with which to show Southern cruelty and disregard for human rights. Southerners, on the other hand, used John Brown's attack on Kansas to show the extreme measures that abolitionists would take.

As Sojourner continued to travel, her passion against slavery gave her the energy to continue attacking it as inhuman, unchristian, and intolerable. She was not always kind or moderate. Sometimes she gave vent to her anger when she thought about what slavery had done. On one occasion, she declared, "All the gold in California, all the wealth of this nation could not restore to me that which the white people have taken from me." Although Sojourner spoke to white people, she never diluted her criticism and opposition to the white people who had enslaved her and her fellow blacks.

When Sojourner was sixty years old, she decided it was time to retire and enjoy the life she'd dreamed of for years. In 1857, she sold her Northampton house for $750 and moved to Harmonia, Michigan, a short distance from Battle Creek.

Sojourner's daughter Elizabeth Banks also moved to

Harmonia along with her son Sammy. They were joined by Diana and her husband, Jacob Corbin, who was a hotel clerk. They had one son, Frank.

In 1857, fifty-four other African Americans lived in the Battle Creek area, and the mayor was a conductor on the Underground Railroad. The people in the town felt pleased and honored to have such a famous person as Sojourner Truth living among them. They helped her change an old barn on College Street into a comfortable house. There she planned to spend her final days enjoying her grandchildren.

From the beginning, Sammy Banks, Elizabeth's son from her second marriage, favored his grandmother. He begged to stay with her, and Sojourner welcomed his companionship. When he was young, Sammy ran errands and did various chores for his grandmother. Then when Sammy learned to read, he read the Bible to Sojourner. In many ways, Sammy became a substitute for Sojourner's lost son, Peter.

For days, Sojourner was content to sit on the front porch, telling stories and singing hymns. But just as Sojourner was settling down into retirement, the Supreme Court placed still another wedge in the gulf between the North and the South. Dred Scott, a slave, had sued for his freedom because he had lived in a free state. The court considered the case in 1857 and determined that a slave was "property" and therefore not a citizen. They said that Scott didn't have the right to sue. This decision was a blow to the abolitionists, but it didn't really affect Scott. His "owner" freed him immediately after the case was final.

When Sojourner Truth learned about the Scott decision, she became convinced that it was not the time to retreat. Against her daughters' protests, Sojourner prepared to begin another speaking tour. Before she left, she had her autobiography updated by her friend and neighbor, Frances Titus, who edited and expanded the narrative six times between 1853 and 1884. Then, taking Sammy with her, sixty-two-year-old Sojourner Truth went back out on the speaking tour.

After traveling for a year, Frances Titus volunteered to become Sojourner's traveling companion and "manager." Together, the two women spoke to anti-slavery groups. Sojourner told audiences, "Slavery must be destroyed, root and branch."

Indiana was a difficult place for abolitionists. While speaking in Kosciusko County with her good friend, Parker Pillsbury, Sojourner experienced a vicious personal attack. A local doctor who led a pro-slavery group claimed Sojourner wasn't a woman. He insisted that she was a man impersonating a woman.

"We demand," the leader said, "if it be a she, that she expose one of her breasts to the gaze of some of the ladies present so that they may report back and dispel the audience's doubts."

Pillsbury leaped to his friend's defense, but Sojourner stopped him asking, "Why do you suppose me to be a man?"

"It's your voice," the doctor said. "Your voice is not that of a woman." After a moment of hesitation, Sojourner began to slowly unbutton her blouse. "I will show my breast," she said to the astonishment of the audience, "but to the entire congregation. It is not to my shame but yours that I do this."

At another time, the people told Sojourner that they would burn down the meeting hall where she was scheduled to speak. Without fear or hesitation, she replied, "I'll speak on the ashes."

During her travels, Sojourner did more than simply speak before large audiences. Harriet Beecher Stowe wrote in "Libyan Sibyl" about an incident that happened in the Stowes' residence. "There was at the time an invalid in the house, and Sojourner, on learning it, felt a mission to go and comfort her. It was curious to see the tall, gaunt, dusky figure stalk up to the bed with such an air of conscious authority, and take on herself the office of consoler with such a mixture of authority and tenderness."

On that particular trip, Sojourner had grown older. It was difficult for her to get started in the morning. "But once she gets up," it was said, "she can go as long as a woman half her age." Another observer noticed that though Sojourner had aged, "There was both power and sweetness in that great warm soul and that vigorous frame." Much as her hard life was affecting her health, she was still able to keep the crowd on the edges of their seats to catch her every word.

NINE

Between 1800 and 1859, bold black leaders led at least two hundred slave uprisings. Three different leaders were prominent during this period: Gabriel Prosser, Denmark Vesey, and Nat Turner.

Merely mentioning those names to slaveholders was to strike fear into their hearts. In 1800, Prosser had organized and armed slaves who were prepared to take Richmond, Virginia, by force. Before Prosser could carry out his plan, however, he was betrayed and hanged. In 1822, Vesey, a free black man, recruited nine thousand slaves to take part in an attack on Charleston, South Carolina. He, too, was betrayed and hanged along with many of his followers. Then in 1831, Turner, a Virginia slave, led a revolt where sixty whites were killed. The authorities captured Turner and hanged him, as well.

The people who lived in the South knew that blacks

outnumbered whites three to one, so they had reason to worry about rebellions. A female relative of George Washington put it simply: "We know that death in the most horrid form threatens us." Such fear may be part of the reason why slaves received swift and severe punishment for any form of disloyalty to their masters.

Sojourner argued that slave masters had much more to fear than slave insurrections. "It is God the slave owner will answer to on the day of judgment."

While Prosser, Vesey, and Turner caused a rip in the fabric of American politics, John Brown's 1859 raid on Harpers Ferry, Virginia, (now West Virginia) caused a great upheaval. Since the Kansas border wars, Brown had become a radical who advocated an armed attack against the South to free the slaves and train them as soldiers to free other slaves. Often Brown said that slaveholders had "forfeited their right to live."

Brown planned to capture arms at the military arsenal at Harpers Ferry, then free slaves through force. But the plan failed. Brown was captured and hanged on December 2, 1859.

Although Sojourner was illiterate, her grandson, Sammy kept her well informed about the political affairs of the day. Sammy read aloud every detail of Brown's trial and execution. Southerners accused Brown of being a maniacal murderer, and at first, more than a few moderate abolitionists tried to distance themselves from Brown's firebrand methods. But the grassroots support for Brown was overwhelming. While Brown represented only a small faction of the movement during his life, every abolitionist embraced him in death. Brown became a martyred folk hero, a symbol to the cause of freedom. The song "John Brown's Body" was written about him and became extremely popular. It was a personal favorite of Abraham Lincoln. Later, during the Civil War, Julia Ward Howe wrote "The Battle Hymn of the Republic" to the music of "John Brown's Body."

Sammy also kept his grandmother informed about the upcoming presidential election. Sojourner was particularly interested in Abraham Lincoln and the new Republican Party. She asked her grandson to read articles about Lincoln whenever he found them. Sojourner liked what she learned about the former Illinois congressman and his stance on slavery.

During a debate with Senator Douglas in 1858, Lincoln proclaimed, "A house divided against itself cannot stand! I believe this government cannot endure permanently half slave and half free. I do not expect the Union to be dissolved; I do not expect the house to fall; but I do expect it will cease to be divided. It will become all one thing or all the other." When Lincoln was a congressman, he introduced a bill providing for the gradual emancipation of slaves in Washington, D.C. He opposed the opening of territories to slavery, and he spoke out against the Dred Scott decision. Sojourner was convinced that Lincoln would be a good president but waited to endorse him.

Most abolitionists were being cautious about Lincoln

because he hadn't called for the immediate elimination of slavery. Fiercely defending its right to treat people as property, the South threatened to establish its own slave-holding nation if Lincoln was elected president.

When Lincoln won the presidency in the November election, a wide-scale rebellion broke out in the South. By February 1861, seven states had broken off from the Union and formed a Confederate government. Four of the other eight slave states soon joined the Confederacy, and the North and South prepared for war. On April 12, 1861, the Civil War broke out when Confederate units attacked Union troops stationed at Fort Sumter, in Charleston, South Carolina.

Sojourner was in Michigan when she got word that a rebel general had fired on Fort Sumter. She hadn't wanted a war; but once it started, she gave her full support to the Union soldiers. Like Frederick Douglass, Sojourner was concerned that blacks weren't given an opportunity to fight for their freedom. The anti-slavery society and the blacks hailed the war as a struggle to end slavery, but many Americans viewed it as chiefly a battle to reunite the country. Early in the war, Union armies suffered a string of defeats, and anger about even being in a war ran high in many areas of the North.

Immediately after the battle at Fort Sumter, many blacks volunteered for service, but they were turned away. As the war progressed, Lincoln was bombarded with requests from black and white leaders to create a "colored unit," and to allow blacks to serve in ways other than as cooks and laborers.

During the fall of 1862, Lincoln finally yielded to the pressure and ordered an all-black unit to be established with white officers. The 54th Massachusetts Volunteer Infantry was a "test" for the black soldier's ability in combat. Would these blacks run under fire? Would they follow orders from their officers? Could they be disciplined? The men of the 54th proved that they could be excellent combat soldiers.

The African American response to the 54th was phenomenal. From all over the country, young blacks came to Boston and signed up. Two of Douglass's sons joined, along with nineteen-year-old James Caldwell, one of Sojourner's grandsons. Her only regret was that she couldn't join herself. James, she said, had "gone forth to redeem the white people from the curse that God has sent upon them. . . . I'd be on hand as the Joan of Arc, to lead the army of the Lord, for now is the day and the hour for the colored man to save his nation."

Sojourner Truth decided to make a tour of the Midwest and rouse support for the Union's war effort. As Sojourner traveled on this speaking tour, angry mobs greeted her in some places and bands of supporters in others. The anti-war and anti-black feelings ran especially high in Indiana, where the state legislature had passed a law forbidding blacks from entering the state. Sojourner defied the law and campaigned throughout the state for the Union cause. She was arrested numerous times. On each occasion, friendly crowds gathered to defend her with shouts of "Sojourner, free speech, and the Union!"

The rigors of such conflict exhausted Sojourner, and she returned home to recover. To have her immediate family nearby served as a great source of comfort to Sojourner, but it also meant that each of her children were free from the bonds of slavery.

Despite her feelings of comfort, Sojourner still had to find the means to support herself financially. In her sixties, she could no longer do the strenuous work of cleaning and cooking for people in Battle Creek. Nor could she continue selling her armloads of books at anti-slavery conventions. Her years of such work had weakened her.

Josephine Griffing, a feminist and abolitionist friend of Sojourner's, came to visit her in Michigan. For the better part of a year, Josephine and Sojourner had traveled throughout Ohio sharing hardships and triumphs.

"I've come to beg your help," Griffing said. "As you know, the president promised to free the slaves the first part of the year. The war effort is not going well. . .anti-slavery speakers are needed more than ever to rally people to our cause. I have been asked to go into Indiana, and I want you to come with me."

Sojourner smiled and said, "Let me get my hat."

Throughout the rest of 1862, Josephine and Sojourner traveled together and urged people to push for the end of slavery. In the *National Anti-Slavery Standard* in New York, Josephine wrote an article, which said in part, "Our meetings are largely attended by persons from every part of the country. . . . Slavery made a conquest in this country by the suppression of free speech, and freedom must make her conquest by the steadfast support of free speech. There are a hundred men now who would spill their blood sooner than surrender the rights of Sojourner."

During one of Sojourner's lectures, a lawyer stood and ranted about how blacks were nothing more than apes or baboons. Sojourner managed to bring the audience's wrath on the lawyer when she replied, "Children, I am one of those monkey tribes. . . . I am going to reply to this creature. Now in the course of my time I have done a great deal of dirty scullion work, but of all the dirty work I have ever done, this is the scullionest and the dirtiest. Now, children, don't you pity me?"

At other times, Sojourner addressed her audience with gentleness. She addressed the Children's Mass Meeting at the Methodist Church during the Annual State Sabbath Convention in 1863. Facing a young, all-white audience, she said, "Children, who made your skin white? Was it not God? Who made mine black? Was it not the same God? Now, children, remember what Sojourner Truth has told you, and thus get rid of your prejudice and learn to love colored children, that you may be all the children of your Father in heaven."

Articles reporting on Sojourner's "lectures" and other activities that supported the abolitionist cause often made references to her encounters with "Negro haters" and "mobocrats." These loud-voiced opponents of black freedom tried repeatedly to disrupt her meetings and drown out her truths. Some of these conflicts were described by eyewitnesses, and others were just hinted at by writers.

As Sojourner traveled through Indiana with her friend Josephine Griffing, Sojourner and her friends were arrested several times. Sojourner was arrested for entering the state, and her friends were arrested for welcoming her into their homes. In each case, Sojourner managed to outwit the authorities or shame them into releasing her. At one point Union soldiers had to protect her from arrest by the local police; another time, prosecution lawyers came to the courtroom drunk. They took one look at the influential crowd around Sojourner and left again, to be seen crossing the street to the tavern.

Often Sojourner's meetings in Indiana were disrupted with loud and insulting shouts such as, "Down with you! We think the niggers have done enough! We will not hear you speak! Stop your mouth!"

At one meeting, the situation became so dangerous that Sojourner's friends dressed her in military clothing in order to put the fear of God into her enemies. Later she recalled the experience saying, "The ladies thought I should be dressed in uniform as well as the captain of the home guard. So they put upon me a red, white, and blue shawl, a sash and apron to match, a cap on my head with a star in the front and a star on each shoulder. When I was dressed, I looked in the glass and was fairly frightened. Said I, 'It seems I am goin' to battle.' My friends advised me to take a sword or pistol. I replied, 'I carry no weapon; the Lord will preserve me without weapons. I feel safe even in the midst of my enemies; for the truth is powerful and will prevail.'"

Sojourner was taken to the meeting in a carriage and surrounded by an army of soldiers. A mob was gathered around the courthouse where she was scheduled to speak. When they saw the crowd of supporters following Sojourner's carriage, they quickly left, described by some as "looking like a flock of frightened crows." No one was left but a small boy who sat on a fence crying, "Nigger, nigger!" The meeting went as planned without interruption.

On January 1, 1863, President Abraham Lincoln signed an executive order ending slavery in the rebel states. The Emancipation Proclamation read, "All persons held as slaves within any State, or designated part of a State the people whereof shall then be in rebellion against the United States, shall be then, thenceforward, and forever free."

The proclamation was received across the North with cheers and tears. Thousands of churches rang their church bells. People danced in the streets. Sojourner gathered her friends in Battle Creek and celebrated with cheering, singing, and long speeches. In her mind, no Pinxter festival could compare to the joy and enthusiasm that people shared who had dedicated their lives to freedom.

Several days after the emancipation, Sojourner had a stroke. Somehow the rumor spread that she had died.

The editor at the *Anti-Slavery Standard,* Oliver Johnson, believed the rumor and printed a story about her death. Author Harriet Beecher Stowe wrote about her 1853 meeting with Sojourner and Sojourner's accomplishments as a tribute to her life. The article was published in the April 1863 issue of *Atlantic Monthly* magazine. People who had never heard of Sojourner were introduced to the amazing exploits of the woman who Stowe called the "The Libyan (African) Sibyl," which referred to a prophetess from ancient times. Stowe was amazed at Sojourner's great intellectual abilities and wondered what other feats this illiterate former slave would have accomplished if she had learned how to read and write.

But the great lady wasn't dead. With the help of her friends and family, Sojourner recovered quickly. Imagine the surprised look on Harriet Stowe's face when she received a thank-you letter from Sojourner!

Sojourner had been active all of her life, and it was almost impossible for her to sit still. Besides, now was no time for a seasoned abolitionist to quit. Sojourner plunged back into her work, even though her daughters urged her at least to slow down. "There's a war going on," Sojourner said, "and I mean to be a part of it."

After the Emancipation Proclamation was issued, the North began to recruit blacks to serve in racially segregated units. Fifteen hundred black troops enlisted in the 1st Michigan Volunteer Black Infantry. These black soldiers weren't paid the same as whites, and sometimes their white officers mistreated them. Sojourner spoke out against this injustice, pointing out that if black soldiers were dying equally, why weren't they paid equally for living?

By Thanksgiving of 1863, Sojourner received the news that her grandson, James Caldwell, was missing in action. He had not been seen since the morning of July 16, 1863, when the 54th had seen action on Majes Island. Two days later, the regiment had attacked Fort Wagner, South Carolina. From the *Standard*, Sammy had read the details to Sojourner: "The Charleston papers all say that 650 of our dead were buried on the Sunday morning after the assault. . . . Unofficial reports say the Negroes have been sold into slavery and that white officers are treated with unmeasurable abuse."

What about James? Truth wondered. *Is he lying in a common grave with others, or is he suffering a fate worse than death—slavery?*

Sojourner traveled to Camp Ward, an army base located near Detroit, Michigan. Over fifteen hundred black troops were stationed at Camp Ward. Truth brought food donated from the residents of Battle Creek so the soldiers could enjoy a proper Thanksgiving dinner. When she arrived, the regiment's commanding officer ordered his men to stand at attention. Then Sojourner spoke to the men about patriotism, and when she finished, the men gave her a rousing cheer. One man told her that she was foolish for trying to help. She asked who he was. He answered, "I am the only son of my mother."

Sojourner replied, "I'm glad there are no more!"

After the official ceremony, Sojourner remained to help prepare the Thanksgiving meal, and while the men ate, she sang a hymn that she'd composed especially for the Michigan Infantry to be sung to the tune of "John Brown's Body":

We are the hardy soldiers of the
*   First of Michigan;*
We're fighting for the union and
*   for the rights of man.*
And when the battle wages
*   you'll find us in the van,*
As we go marching on.

We are the valiant soldiers who
*   'listed for the war;*
We are fighting for the Union;
*   we are fighting for the law.*
We can shoot a rebel farther than
*   a white man ever saw;*
As we go marching on.

They will have to pay us wages,
*   the wages of their sin;*
They will have to bow their foreheads
*   to their colored kith and kin;*
They will have to give us houseroom,
*   or the roof will tumble in,*
As we go marching on.

The bespectacled elderly woman moved from soldier to soldier and served them a proper Thanksgiving dinner. She talked with them about parents and home. "Can you write, son?" she asked a soldier. "Yes," came the response. Sojourner quickly continued, "Have you sent your folks word of your whereabouts?" If the soldier responded, "No," Truth admonished him saying, "Don't grieve your parents. Write them now."

During the spring of 1864, Sojourner decided to visit President Lincoln in Washington, D.C. Although many of her abolitionist friends believed President Lincoln was moving too slowly to bring about an end to slavery, Sojourner greatly respected the president. "Have patience!" she told her friends. "It takes a great while to turn about this great ship of state." In the meantime, she believed that Lincoln could use some encouragement.

Until the day of her departure, Sojourner didn't tell anyone about her plans. She was working as a laundress for a Battle Creek family. "I've got to hurry with this washing," she told her employers. When they asked why she was so pressed for time, she replied, "Because I'm leaving for Washington this afternoon. I'm going down there to advise the president."

Accompanied by her grandson, Sammy Banks, Sojourner boarded the train for the nation's capital, stopping in several towns along the route to give speeches. In September 1864, she reached Washington, D.C. In a little more than a month, Americans would vote about whether President Lincoln would serve a second term of office.

At last Sojourner and Sammy reached the nation's capital. When she saw the flag, she whispered to him, "No more scars and stripes, just stars and stripes for all God's children."

Parts of Washington reminded her of the Five Points district in New York City. The streets of Washington were filled with slaves who had poured into the city after their freedom. They lived in unhealthy conditions and were surrounded by despair and filth. Sojourner's heart went out to them, and she helped them whenever she could.

Freeing the slaves had created another problem: What was to be done with the millions of people who had no education or money and only limited skills? Congress had set aside funds to establish the Freedman's Bureau, which was designed to help freed slaves make the transition from slavery to freedom. Sojourner hoped that there might be some job for her within the Bureau.

When Sojourner learned that her good friend and former traveling companion, Josephine Griffing, was in Washington, she went to see her right away. Griffing had become the local agent of the National Freedman's Relief Association. When Sojourner expressed her concerns about the condition of the newly freed slaves, Josephine said, "I know just the place for you: Freedman's Village."

Constructed by the army as a model village: Freedman's Village was a series of neat cottages, a great improvement over the shacks the slaves had lived in during slavery. The village was located in Arlington, Virginia, just outside Washington, on the old estate of General Robert E. Lee.

Sojourner, along with her grandson Sammy, moved into the village. In November, she dictated a letter to her friend Amy Post in Rochester:

"I am at Freedman's Village. . . . I judge it is the will of both God and people that I should remain. Ask Mr. Oliver Johnson to please send me the *Standard* while I'm here, as many of the colored people like to hear what is going on and know what is being done for them. Sammy, my grandson, reads for them."

In the village, Sojourner moved around like a woman half her age. She helped the other women learn how to sew, cook, clean, comb hair, and take care of their children. She sent Sammy to the village school and encouraged mothers not only to send their children but also to attend adult classes themselves.

One day Sojourner found a group of women huddled together, frightened and crying. White men had stolen their children and made them work without pay. "Fight the robbers," Sojourner told them forcefully. "You're free now. Don't let anyone treat you like slaves!"

Sojourner remembered how she had used the law to get Peter back from Gedney. She helped the women use the law to get their children back. One of the white men, who was from Maryland, tried to intimidate her with threats. "Old woman," he growled, "stay out of our affairs, or we'll put you in jail."

The words didn't budge the seasoned warrior. She told him, "If you try anything like that, I shall make the United States rock like a cradle." The men left Sojourner alone and stopped raiding the Freedman's Village to steal children.

Although Sojourner had been in Washington, D.C., several weeks, she still hadn't gotten a chance to meet with President Lincoln. When she'd first arrived, she'd tried to secure an appointment with Lincoln but had found that on her own, she was unable to do so. Then she asked Lucy Colman—a white, Massachusetts-born abolitionist, whose permanent home was in Rochester and who at the time was teaching freed slaves in Washington—to arrange an appointment for her. Colman admired Sojourner, once saying that Truth never "disgraced" her name, and was willing to help her. After some time, Colman, using Mrs. Lincoln's black dressmaker, Elizabeth Keckley, as a go-between, succeeded in arranging an appointment. When Colman finally took Sojourner to the White House on October 29, 1864, the two women had to wait several hours until it was their turn to see the busy president.

From time to time as the women waited, the president appeared to usher someone into his office. Truth was pleased to see that he treated his black guests with the same courtesy that he showed to the white visitors.

Finally, Truth gained her turn to go into the president's office. She had planned to speak with him about improving the conditions of former slaves; but when she was introduced to the president, she looked at his weary face and his shoulders, which seemed to sag heavily with the burden they carried. Sojourner's heart was moved by the great sadness of this man who had freed her people. She decided not to add yet another complaint to his load. Instead, she kept the conversation light.

After she had sat down, Sojourner told him bluntly, "I never heard of you before you were put in for president."

Lincoln laughed at the comment and replied, "I heard of you years and years before I ever thought of being president. Your name is well-known in the Midwest."

President Lincoln showed her around his office and pointed out a Bible that a group of Baltimore blacks had presented to him. She held the book in her hands and traced the big gold letters—the Bible—with her finger. Although Sojourner couldn't read the Book, she knew many of the words in it by heart.

Remembering one of her favorite Bible stories, Sojourner reminded President Lincoln that he was like Daniel in the lions' den; but with God on his side he'd win, just like Daniel. Then she told the president that in her opinion, he was the best president that the country had ever had.

The president objected to her opinion, saying that Washington, Jefferson, and Adams were greater. "They may have been good to others," Sojourner replied, "but they neglected to do anything for my race. Washington had a good name, but his name didn't reach to us."

Then Sojourner thanked the president for his efforts

to help black Americans and advised him not to worry about the blustering attacks of his critics. The people in the nation were behind him and would support him in the upcoming election, she said. Lincoln, in turn, thanked her for the encouragement. When it was time to leave, Sojourner asked Lincoln to sign her "Book of Life." For Sojourner, the "Book of Life" was a combination scrapbook and autograph book. Throughout her travels, she collected the signatures of the great people she had met and respected. She also kept personal letters and newspaper clippings. Everywhere Sojourner went, she took her "Book of Life" with her.

She watched with great pride as the president signed, "For Aunty Sojourner Truth, A. Lincoln, October 29, 1864." (Years later, the terms "Aunty" and "Uncle" became words that black women and men resented. During the time of Lincoln, however, they were terms of endearment. For instance, General William T. Sherman was affectionately known as "Uncle Billy," and General Robert E. Lee's soldiers called him "Uncle Bobby.")

In November, as Sojourner had predicted, Lincoln was swept back into office by an overwhelming margin in the wake of several victories by the Union army. By that time, Sojourner had discovered that she enjoyed the busy atmosphere in the nation's capital. Instead of returning to Battle Creek, she decided to stay in Washington, D.C., and see what she could do to assist the Union's war effort.

At the invitation of prominent black minister Henry Highland Garnet, Sojourner spoke at a local charity benefit to help raise money for black soldiers. In addition, she joined a group of women who were feeding and nursing thousands of former slaves who had fled the South. Many of the escaped slaves settled in Washington, D.C., which had become a free area in April 1862 after Lincoln had signed a bill that outlawed slavery in the capital.

These recently freed slaves endured harsh conditions in Washington. The men and women covered themselves with rags to keep warm in the winter, and they ate scraps gleaned from garbage dumps to keep from starving. Many of them became sick and died.

Besides their physical living conditions, freed slaves also had to hide from the bands of slave traders who kidnapped blacks and smuggled them into the Confederate states. The kidnappers threatened to kill anyone who gave information about the illegal slave trade to the federal marshals. Most freedmen were afraid to say anything in protest.

Sojourner, however, refused to be silenced. She marched through the freedmen's villages and told the freed slaves, "The law is for you. Take refuge in it."

As she attacked the injustices for blacks in the nation's capital, the morale of the African American community rose. Toward the end of 1864, a public welfare organization called the National Freedman's Relief Association asked Sojourner to work as a counselor to former slaves who were living at a camp in Arlington Heights, Virginia. There she educated the freedmen about the need to locate work and housing and about the other responsibilities that came with their newly won freedom.

In February 1865, a journalist named Tomkins found Sojourner working in the basement of Calvary Baptist Church, which the National Freedmen's Relief Association of New York used for clothing distribution. Among several hundred black women who were pushing forward to pick up clothing, Tomkins found Truth in charge, "an erect, tall, aged black woman, neatly clad, wearing a pair of gold spectacles. She was reproving her dark-skinned sisters for their eager haste to obtain relief," Tomkins wrote. " 'You have your liberty,' exclaimed the good old woman, 'but what's your liberty without regulation; by your thoughtless eagerness you hinder your friends relieving you as quickly as they would.' She scolded the women severely: 'I have spoken to some of you before about this foolish haste, and now I say to you the words of the fable, that having tried what turf will do, if that fail, the next time I shall try stones.' " The journalist asked her if she found these people difficult to manage. She answered, "Lord bless you, child, no—they are as gentle as lambs, but they must be brought under rule and regulation. Ah! Poor things; they all have to learn."

Sojourner was still working at the Freedman's Village when General Robert E. Lee surrendered to General

Ulysses S. Grant at Appomattox Courthouse in Virginia on April 9, 1865. The surrender ended the war, leaving more than half a million people dead.

Six days after the surrender, President Lincoln's name was added to the list of victims. A freezing drizzle was falling on Washington the night it was announced that Lincoln had been assassinated during a play at the Ford Theater. Actor John Wilkes Booth had shot the president. Although Lincoln was taken to the home of William Peterson at 453 Tenth Street, he died at 7:22 the next morning.

That same evening in a separate incident, Secretary of State William Seward was stabbed, but he survived. Vice President Andrew Johnson became president of the United States. Sojourner, believing that no one had done more for the cause of black Americans than Lincoln, was devastated by his sudden death.

Sojourner and Sammy joined thousands of people who walked through the East Room of the White House where Lincoln's body lay in state. For the last time, Sojourner looked at the president who would be remembered as "the Emancipator."

In the month following Lincoln's death, the last of the Confederate armies surrendered to Union forces. The Civil War was over. It had spanned four years and taken hundreds of thousands of lives, but the battle against slavery had been won. Sojourner's prayers had been answered. She had lived to see the end of slavery.

On December 12, 1865, Sojourner and millions of other Americans celebrated as Congress ratified the Thirteenth Amendment to the Constitution. It declared that "Neither slavery, nor involuntary servitude. . .shall exist within the United States, or any place subject to their jurisdiction." At last, slavery had officially ended.

Returning to the Freedman's Village, Sojourner spent hours trying to convince former slaves that Lincoln's death didn't mean reenslavement and that Vice President Johnson, from Tennessee, wouldn't turn back the clock of time. Even though Sojourner sounded convincing, she had her private doubts.

During the summer of 1865, she met with President Andrew Johnson. "Please be seated, Mrs. Truth," said the president.

"Sit down yourself, Mr. President," Sojourner replied. "I'm used to standing because I've been lecturing for many years." Then she talked with the president about her concerns and the problems that her people faced, based on firsthand information from Freedman's Village. While the president listened politely, he made no commitment. Sojourner carried her "Book of Life" that day, but she didn't ask President Johnson to sign it. She never explained whether it was oversight or intention.

Not long after her visit with Johnson, the War Department assigned Sojourner to work at the Freedman's Hospital. They needed her to help "promote order, cleanliness, industry, and virtue among the patients." Although Sojourner was seventy years old, she accepted the position. She did her best to ensure that proper medical care was given to the hospital's black patients. Her booming voice could be heard throughout the halls of the hospital: "Be clean! Be clean!" Her work gave her a renewed sense of purpose, and she began to have greater energy than she had for some time.

Since Sammy was helping at the Freedman's Village, he and Sojourner continued to live there. Also, he continued to keep in communication with the family back in Battle Creek. By this time, Sojourner's grandson James had returned home from the Civil War. He had survived months as a prisoner of war.

To get to and from her work at the hospital, Sojourner often walked; but one day she decided to take a streetcar. She signaled a car to stop. When it kept going, she ran after it, yelling. The conductor kept ringing his bell so that he could pretend that he had not heard her. When at last the conductor had to stop the car to take on white passengers, Sojourner climbed into the car, scolding the conductor, "It is a shame to make a lady run so." He replied that if she said another word to him, he would put her off. She threatened him, "If you attempt that, it will cost you more than your car and horses are worth." When a dignified man in the uniform of a general interfered on her behalf, the conductor left her alone.

Sojourner was keenly aware that the law was on her side. She did not try to organize blacks to join her, but when circumstances seemed to suggest it, she acted directly and on her own.

In another incident, Sojourner held up her hand to signal a car to stop. Two cars passed by without stopping. When a third car came into sight, she yelled, "I want to ride! I want to ride! *I want to ride!*" Her shouting startled enough nearby horses, drivers, pedestrians, and boys pushing carts to block traffic, which stopped the car. That hesitation gave Sojourner the chance to climb into the car, to the laughter of some of the other passengers. Some of them called out to the conductor, "She has beaten you."

The conductor was furious and told her to go up front, outside with the driver. But Sojourner sat down with the other passengers. He told her to get up or be thrown out. She told the conductor, "Throw me out if you dare" for she was "neither a Marylander nor a Virginian" but "from the Empire State of New York, and I know the laws as well as you do."

At least one of the passengers in the car, a soldier, seemed to sympathize with her. As new passengers came in, he exclaimed to them delightedly, "You ought to have heard that old woman talk to the conductor." Sojourner herself was so pleased to be riding in the car that she rode farther than she had intended, and when she left, said happily, "Bless God! I have had a ride."

Once Sojourner was bringing a black nurse from Georgetown to the Freedman's Hospital. The nurse was uneasy about riding the streetcar with whites. Nevertheless, Sojourner led the nurse to an empty streetcar that was preparing to leave, and they seated themselves. After the car proceeded on its way, it stopped for two white women, who came in and sat opposite the two black women. These two white women began to whisper about Sojourner and her companion. Truth noticed them staring at her with great hostility. The nurse finding herself on a level with white women for the first time hung her head down toward her lap, but Sojourner looked fearlessly about. At length, one of the white women called out in a weak, faint voice, "Conductor, conductor, do niggers ride in these cars?"

He hesitatingly answered, "Yes," to which she responded, "This is a shame and a disgrace. They ought to have a nigger car on the track."

At that point, Sojourner spoke up. "Of course colored people ride in the cars. Streetcars are designed for poor white and colored folks. Carriages are for ladies and gentlemen. There are carriages standing ready to take you three or four miles for sixpence, and then you talk of a nigger car!" On hearing this, the women left the streetcar in a huff, presumably to take a more expensive and more exclusive mode of transportation.

"Ah!" Sojourner said, "now they are going to take a carriage. Good-bye, ladies."

A few weeks later, Sojourner and her white friend, Mrs. Laura Haviland, were boarding a streetcar together. Sojourner stepped ahead of her friend, but the conductor snatched her out of the way. "Let the lady on before you," he snapped.

"I'm a lady, too," Sojourner snapped back. The conductor pushed Sojourner off the streetcar.

Mrs. Haviland stopped the man. "Don't you put her off," she said.

"Why? Does she belong to you?" the conductor asked angrily.

"No," Mrs. Haviland replied. "She belongs to humanity."

"Then take her and go!" The conductor slammed Sojourner against the door and bruised her shoulder. After Sojourner asked Haviland to jot down the number of the car, the conductor left them alone. "It is hard for the old slaveholding spirit to die," Sojourner reflected, "but die it must."

Back at the hospital, when the two women asked a surgeon to examine Sojourner's shoulder, he found it swollen. Then the two women reported the incident to the president of the streetcar company. He promptly fired the conductor.

This company president also advised Sojourner to have the conductor arrested for assault, which she did with the help of the Freedman's Bureau, who furnished her with a lawyer. A few days later, Justice William Thompson held a hearing for the conductor, as reported in a curious article published in at least four Washington newspapers.

Sojourner won her case in court. As she said about the incident, "Before the trial was over, so many blacks were now daring to ride in the cars that the inside of the cars looked like pepper and salt." Soon the conductors who had cursed Sojourner for wanting to ride would stop for both black and white ladies and even conde-scend to say, "Walk in, ladies." Sojourner later claimed that her Washington ride-ins had changed the city. The old warrior marked another victory in her struggle for equality.

TEN

Sojourner's victory over the streetcars, however, was short-lived. Soon laws were passed across the nation that made it illegal for blacks and whites to ride together. These "Jim Crow" laws stayed in force until the modern civil rights movement.

Meanwhile, Sojourner continued speaking out about women's rights. When she addressed an audience, Frederick Douglass said, "She seemed to please herself and others best when she put her ideas in the oddest forms." In 1867, she complained to a New York newspaperman that he was not reporting her words accurately, but she admitted "good-naturedly," he said, that her speech was difficult to record because she "was speaking in an unknown tongue."

Largely, Sojourner spoke from her own experiences, but what she said reflected an awareness of the current clash of thought. She was able to cut through the debate with startling flashes of insight. She was very articulate, even though not in as ordered a fashion as Douglass. Her thinking was more spontaneous. It lent itself to sudden leaps, poetry, and parable.

Sojourner spoke extemporaneously, she said, not knowing what the Lord would put into her mouth. Some phrases she spoke deliberately, while others she raced through. Often she interrupted herself with droll asides. According to a Quaker friend, Sojourner had a "magnetic power over an audience." The *Detroit Advertiser* wrote that she "had a heart of love" and a "tongue of fire." Her friend Lucy Stone said that Sojourner spoke "with direct and terrible force, moving friend and foe alike."

In other aspects of her life, illiteracy continued to handicap Sojourner. Once she conceded that it was "hard work" to get as many letters written for her as she wanted. In another instance, thanking a correspondent for "her kind words," she replied as a friend wrote down her response, "Oh, if I could but write and answer them myself." More importantly, Sojourner's illiteracy limited her opportunities for leadership. She never became part of the decision-making inner circles of either the abolitionists or women's rights movement as Frederick Douglass sometimes did. Also, her illiteracy kept Sojourner poor because it limited her job opportunities. But her overwhelming faith that God had called her to a special mission to set the world right side up seemed to convince Sojourner that her illiteracy was another God-given trait, like her blackness and womanhood, which fashioned her beautifully to carry out her mission.

Whenever Sojourner spoke, she usually sang— sometimes with difficulty as she grew older. At an 1867 equal rights convention in New York, she said she had not heard any singing at the convention, but "there ought to be singing here." Though she admitted, "I can't sing as well as I used to," she proceeded to sing, and the audience responded with hearty applause. One newspaper reporter at the conference reported on the singing as "a weird, wailing song, with a very queer tune, an odd though clear pronunciation of words, and her old head swaying to and fro in harmony." The song that she sang twice to the same convention, Sojourner called one of her favorites:

> We are going home;
>   we have visions bright
> Of that holy land,
>   that world of light
> Where the dark night is past,
>   And the morning of eternity has come at last.
> Where the weary saints
>   no more shall roam,
> But dwell in a sunny
>   and peaceful home.
> Where the brow
>   celestial gems shall crown
> And waves of bliss
>   are dashing round.

Oh! What a beautiful home—
Oh! that beautiful world.

The next year, Sojourner sang the same song to six hundred listeners at a Progressive Friends meeting in Erie County, New York. Though she was about seventy-one years old at the time, one listener reported that she sang this song, "in a steady, clear voice, which we know fell like a sacred baptism upon all hearts present."

For years, abolitionists and women's rights activists had worked together and supported each other's cause. In 1869, the Fifteenth Amendment to the Constitution was passed, giving black men the right to vote, but women were still excluded. It said, "The right of citizens of the United States to vote shall not be denied or abridged by the United States or by any State on account of race, color, or previous condition of servitude."

Women abolitionists felt betrayed by black men who benefited from their efforts and then seemed to desert them. Even Frederick Douglass, who had been the first to back women's rights to vote, said, "This hour belongs to the Negro."

After hearing this statement, Elizabeth Cady Stanton retorted, "My question is this: Do you believe the African race is composed entirely of males?"

The argument divided women into two different camps. The National Woman Suffrage Association (NWSA), which was founded in 1869 by Elizabeth Cady Stanton and Susan B. Anthony, devoted their efforts to women's suffrage through constitutional amendment. The American Woman Suffrage Association (AWSA), founded a few months later by Lucy Stone and Henry Blackwell, believed women's suffrage was best achieved through state actions.

Each organization looked for allies among the former women's abolitionists. Since Sojourner had always championed the cause of women's suffrage, Susan B. Anthony wrote her a letter with a petition listing demands for women's rights and asked her to sign it. Sojourner responded, "I feel that if I have to answer for the deeds done in my body just as much as a man, I have a right to have just as much as a man. There is a great stir about colored men getting their rights, but not a word about the colored women; and if colored men get their rights, and not colored women theirs, you see the colored men will be masters over the women, and it will be just as bad as it was before. So I am for keeping the thing going while things are stirring; because if we wait till it is still, it will take a great while to get it going again."

Sojourner's prophecy about the future of the women's suffrage movement came true. The movement lost momentum during the next few years. Stanton, Stone, Truth, and others died before women won the right to vote.

Before long, black male voters began to make their numbers felt and increased their representation in state legislatures. In addition, more than twenty black leaders —including Blanche K. Bruce, P. B. S. Pinchback, Joseph Rainey, and Hiram Revels—were elected to Congress during the Reconstruction era. The work of these legislators helped to end more than two hundred years of enforced ignorance as blacks throughout the South began to attend free schools and acquire knowledge that could help them succeed in a free society.

Another theme of Sojourner's speeches during this period was equal pay for equal work. She told her audiences, "I have done a great deal of work, as much as a man, but did not get as much pay. I used to work in the field and bind grain, keeping up with the cradler; but men doing no more, got twice as much pay. . . . We do as much; we eat as much; we want as much."

Then she pointed to the sad fact that she was the only black woman speaking out for black women's rights and begged her listeners to join her. Addressing the men in the crowd, she said, "You have been having our rights so long that you think like a slaveholder that you own us. I know that is hard for one who has held the reins for so long to give up; it cuts like a knife. It will feel all the better when it closes up again."

Sojourner felt strongly about the women's suffrage issue. She not only spoke about it, but she acted on her beliefs. Some report that Sojourner tried to vote for Ulysses S. Grant in 1868. Four years later, in Battle Creek, she attempted to register to vote in the third ward, where she lived. Of course, she was refused, but nevertheless, she appeared the following week on election day and tried to vote. Once again, she was refused, but she remained at the polls all day and lectured the authorities on the issue of women's rights. The newspaper that reported this incident concluded their article, "It is Sojourner's determination to continue the assertion of her rights until she gains them."

Sojourner Truth was absolutely firm in her conviction about her rights as a citizen—whether or not the authorities agreed with her. She could do no less than attempt to exercise her rights. Her insistence about her right to vote moved Elizabeth Cady Stanton to write in Sojourner's "Book of Life": "I hope, dear Sojourner, that you will be enfranchised before you leave us for a better land."

Not only Sojourner's personal feelings inspired her fight to express her political opinion through the ballot. As in her fight for the end of slavery, Sojourner truly believed that she was doing the work of God and that somehow her person and her actions embodied God's will. Thus, when she addressed the equal righters in New York, she declared (perpetuating the myth about her age), "I am above eighty years old; it is about time for me to be going. . . . I suppose I am kept here because something remains for me to do; I suppose I am yet to help to break the chain." Unfortunately she never lived to see women voting. The chain to which she referred didn't break until the ratification of the Nineteenth Amendment, which granted women the right to vote in 1920.

Famous editor Theodore Tilton wanted to write Sojourner's life story. She answered in typical fashion, "I am not ready to be writ up yet, for I have still lots to accomplish."

Although Sojourner Truth was over seventy years old, she took up one more cause—land rights. Besides continuing her ongoing cause of women's rights, she worked for government-sponsored black homesteads out West. Sojourner argued that blacks had been forced to work with no profit from their own labor, yet no slave had ever been compensated. It was too late to pay back with money, but by setting aside land for each slave—"Twenty acres and a mule"—the government, in her opinion, could pay the debt in full.

Sojourner began to talk up the idea of a land-grant program for former slave families. Since farming was what these people knew best, why not provide them with a means to become productive, self-sufficient citizens?

As Sojourner spent more and more time among the freed slaves, she saw their lives had been used for the enrichment of others, their labor had been taken from them, and their children stolen away. She became angry. Looking at the large, white buildings around Washington, she exclaimed, "We helped pay this cost." Then she detailed with painful accuracy the vast and various contributions black people had made to the welfare and development of the United States. She made certain to point out that their efforts were yet to be acknowledged and rewarded.

Later one of Sojourner's friends, Francis Titus, captured her thoughts in this manner, "We have been a source of wealth to this republic. Beneath a burning Southern sun have we toiled, in the canebrake and the rice swamps, urged on by the merciless driver's lash, earning millions of money; and so highly were we valued there that should one poor wretch venture to escape from this hell of slavery, no exertion of man or trained bloodhound was spared to seize and return him to his field of unrequited labor. . . ."

These were bitter words from a woman who had known firsthand the cut of the whip and the backbreaking fieldwork that had enriched the nation. Sojourner knew that the government owned vast lands in the West and was giving many acres to the large and rapidly expanding railroad companies. She wondered why some of these acres could not go to the women and men whose bondage had served to increase the nation's wealth. She didn't ask for all of the land, merely enough on which black people could build the new life they so badly needed.

Sojourner's job at the Freedman's Hospital had finished, so she and Sammy traveled the nation to lecture for equal women's rights and newly freed blacks. Her lectures often succeeded in helping people throw off their prejudice and hatred. As a New Yorker wrote in 1868, "She produced a singular effect upon the audience, melting away the prejudice of color and creed. We have seldom witnessed more marked results upon the Soul of an audience. . . ."

On March 31, 1870, Sojourner returned to Washington, D.C., and along with Giles Stebbins of Detroit, visited the newly elected president, Ulysses S. Grant. Through talking with the president, she hoped to gain support for her land-grant proposal.

As the meeting began, both Sojourner and the president were stiff and very formal with each other, but by the end of the meeting, Sojourner, her eyes glowing with emotion, thanked Grant for his efforts to secure new guarantees of justice for blacks. The president was moved. He replied that he hoped to be wise and firm and to remember that everybody deserved full rights. Then he signed Truth's "Book of Life" and took one of her calling cards as a memento of their meeting.

Later in the *Detroit Tribune*, Stebbins captured the meeting in an article about Sojourner. "She expressed her pleasure in meeting him, yet I could see it was not quite easy on either side. She had met Abraham Lincoln, and he, born a Kentuckian, could call her 'Aunty' in the old familiar way, while Grant was reticent yet kindly. But a happy thought came to her. It was the civil rights bill days, and not long before he had signed some act of Congress giving new guarantees of justice to the colored people. She spoke of this gracefully and the thin ice broke. Standing there, tall and erect while stirred in soul by the occasion, her wonderful eyes glowed with emotion as she thanked him for his good deed to the once enslaved race to which she belonged. . . . Words followed freely on both sides— she telling him how his tasks and trials were appreciated, and how much faith was placed in his upright doing of duty to the oppressed, and he quietly, yet with much feeling, expressing the hope that he might be wise and firm and never forget the unalienable rights of all."

The meeting with Grant capped a memorable pair of days for Sojourner. On the previous day, the Fifteenth Amendment had been ratified, guaranteeing the right to vote for all men regardless of "race, color, or previous condition of servitude." The right to vote was crucial to the welfare of blacks, who made up a sizable portion of the Southern population and composed the majority in some states.

But when the help that Sojourner expected from Grant was not forthcoming, she took her request to Congress. Arriving at the Capitol building one morning dressed in her usual white cap, gray dress, and white shawl, Sojourner cut a striking figure as she addressed a group of senators.

"We have been a source of wealth to this republic," she said, eloquently defending her position. "Our labor supplied the country with cotton, until villages and cities dotted the enterprising North for its manufacture, and furnished employment and support for a multitude, thereby becoming a revenue to the government. . . . Our nerves and sinews, our tears and blood have been sacrificed on the altar of this nation's avarice. Our unpaid labor has been a stepping-stone to its financial success. Some of its dividends must surely be ours."

A reporter captured Sojourner's message to the senators with these words: "It was an hour not soon to be forgotten. It was refreshing, but also strange, to see a woman born in the shackles of slavery now treated to a reception by senators in a marble room. A decade ago she would have been spurned from its outer corridor by the lowest menial. . . . Truly, the spirit of progress is abroad in the land!"

Fourteen senators signed Sojourner's "Book of Life" even though they weren't supportive of her land-grant proposal. Senator Charles Sumner of Massachusetts, however, took more than a casual interest in her ideas. He promised to sponsor a bill if she could show him that there was widespread support for such a plan. Sojourner had the following petition drawn up:

> *To the Senate and House of Representatives, in Congress Assembled:*
>
> *Whereas, from the faithful and earnest representatives of Sojourner Truth (who has personally investigated the matter) we believe that the freed colored people in and about Washington, dependent upon government for support, would be greatly benefited and might become useful citizens by being placed in a position to support themselves;*
>
> *We, the undersigned, therefore earnestly request your honorable body to set apart for them a portion of the public land in the West and erect buildings thereon for the aged and infirm, and otherwise legislate so as to secure the desired results.*

With her petition in hand, Sojourner, her grandson

Sammy, and another grandson set out across the nation to collect signatures.

On January 1, 1871, the eighth anniversary of the Emancipation Proclamation, Sojourner celebrated at Tremont Hall in Boston. She spoke about beginning life in a cellar, suffering beatings with a rod, and enduring other indignities during slavery. She said in part, "Now some people say, 'Let the blacks take care of themselves.' But you've taken everything away from them. They don't have anything left! I say, get the black people out of Washington! Get them off the government! Get the old people out and build them homes in the West where they can feed themselves. Lift up those people and put them there. Teach them to read part of the time, and teach them to work the other part of the time. Do that, and they will soon be a people among you. That is my commission!"

When they heard Sojourner speak, the people gladly signed her petition—even those people who initially opposed the proposal. After listening to her, they were convinced.

While in Massachusetts, she received a letter from her friend Olive Gilbert, the woman who had written her autobiography while they had been in Northampton, Massachusetts.

Dear Sojourner,
My dear friend. A line from my brother received this afternoon speaks of your being at

*Vineland, so I must send you a few lines to say
how pleased I was to hear from you through friend
Amy Post of Rochester, New York. . . . I get a
glimpse of you often through the papers, which fall
upon my spirit like bright rays from the sun. . . . I
rejoice and am proud that you can make your
power felt with so little book–education.*

Sojourner went to visit Olive, who helped her gather more signatures for her petition. She also spoke in Rochester while with Olive, eloquently painting a picture of the degradation in which the capital's black population lived. She went on: "You ask me what to do for them? Do you want a poor old creature who doesn't know how to read to tell educated people what to do? I give you the hint, and you ought to know what to do." Once again she appealed for the granting of land by the government and for her audience's support of her petition.

"You owe it to them," she said to the audience, "because you took away from them all they earned and made them what they are. You take no interest in the colored people. . . . You are the cause of the brutality of these poor creatures, for you are the children of those who enslaved them." Then, recalling how eagerly people in those days helped the poor and oppressed outside of the United States, she said, "You are ready to help the heathen in foreign lands, but you don't care for the heathen right around you. I want you to sign petitions to send to Washington. . . ."

Many of the newspaper reports of her speeches during this period were friendly, but there were some that opposed her support of unpopular causes and mocked her uneducated speech and often unconventional ways. One newspaper in Springfield, New Jersey, referred to Sojourner as "an old Negro mummy," because of her advanced age and claimed that "fifty years ago, she was considered a crazy woman." The reporter strongly criticized the person who brought Sojourner to the church in Springfield to speak, calling him a "pious radical" and complaining, "When respectable churches consent to admit to the houses opened for worship of God every wandering Negro minstrel or street spouter who may profess to have had a peculiar religious experience or have some grievance to redress, they rend themselves justly liable to public ridicule."

Sojourner never grew discouraged in her fight for freedom and women's rights. Not only did she make her own gestures toward exercising her rights, but she also encouraged others to exercise their rights. In 1871, she heard that her friend Nannette Gardner had actually succeed in voting in Detroit. She asked for a written statement from Gardner to substantiate the story, and the letter of response she kept among her treasured autographs and papers until her death:

> *Dear Sojourner—*
> *At your request I record the fact that I suc-*
> *ceeded in registering my name in the First Precinct*

of the Ninth Ward, and on Tuesday, the 4th of
April, cast the first vote for a state officer deposited
in an American ballot box by a woman for the last
half century.

Speaking in Detroit in the campaign for the re-election of President Grant in 1872, Sojourner was about seventy-five years old. She "sang several of her original songs, all of which," according to the newspaper, "were received with applause." When she was speaking in a small Pennsylvania town in 1874, a newspaper reported that Sojourner sang "right sweetly a Negro melody. . . giving just enough of a southern Negro double-demi-semi-quaver to it, to make it interesting."

Another newspaper from Springfield declared, "We do most decidedly dislike the complexion and everything else appertaining to Mrs. Truth, the radical—the renowned, saintly, liberated, oratorical, pious slave. . . . She is a crazy, ignorant, repelling negress, and her guardians would do a Christian act to restrict her entirely to private life."

Despite these attacks, which showed the poorest side of society during this period, Sojourner refused to give up her fight to get land for indigent black people. Her advancing age, precarious health, and the threats and jibes of people notwithstanding, Sojourner continued to travel and preach. She passed through Massachusetts, western New York, Michigan, Kansas, Iowa, Illinois, Missouri, Wisconsin, Washington, Ohio, New

Jersey, and Kentucky during the last ten years of her life. On each of these trips, she met with old and new friends, sang her songs, and continued entertaining and enlightening people on a variety of topics—all connected to the well-being and liberation of black people and women.

A year after leaving Washington, Sojourner returned with a thousand signatures. She hurried to Sumner's office and was told by his secretary that the great senator had recently died. No other person would help Sojourner with her cause. Her hopes of getting a bill introduced into the Senate evaporated. The tide of black progress continued to be blocked by conservative whites. More and more, she began to realize that the battle for black freedom had only begun.

Sojourner fought for abolition, equality, and suffrage, but she also moved into other fields of struggle. Like many feminists and abolitionists, Sojourner was attracted to the temperance movement. This movement called for voluntary abstinence from drinking alcoholic beverages. Many references were made to her speaking before temperance groups, either on this subject or on other questions that interested her. Like other black leaders, Sojourner felt alcohol was fast becoming a serious social problem among poor blacks. She believed that only complete sobriety would enable her people to pull themselves up fully from the mire of a past as slaves.

Chewing tobacco and smoking were also practices that were frowned on by the reformers of this period. On one occasion, when Sojourner was speaking before a

189

temperance group in Kansas, men throughout the audience were chewing tobacco and loudly spitting the brown juice on the floor. Finally unable to contain herself any longer, Sojourner quipped, "When I attended the Methodist Church, we used to kneel down in the house of God during prayers. Now I ask you, how could anyone kneel down on these floors?"

At last, Sojourner decided to return home to Michigan. She missed Battle Creek and her family there, but more importantly, Sammy was ill. At first his condition didn't seem serious, but his fever grew worse along with his cough. Worried about her favorite grandson's illness and suffering with an ulcer on her leg, Sojourner grew depressed. When Sammy died in February 1875, her condition worsened. Sammy hadn't even reached his twenty-fifth birthday. To Sojourner, Sammy's death was worse than losing her son Peter because Sammy had been such a good and faithful companion. She never stopped mourning his death.

No matter what Sojourner did, she couldn't work away her hurt. She missed Sammy terribly and without him felt handicapped. He had read to her, taken care of all her correspondence, and looked after her affairs. She had written to her family that she was going back to Battle Creek to die, but she outlived her grandson by nine years.

Meanwhile, conflict throughout the nation continued. In the South, many whites rebelled against the Reconstruction laws by forming white-supremacist groups such as the Ku Klux Klan, which kidnapped and murdered blacks without fear of punishment. White insurrectionists conspired to overthrow the Southern state governments in which blacks had succeeded in marshaling a great deal of power. Blacks armed themselves and fought back, and Grant was forced to send regiments of federal troops to South Carolina and other troubled areas to restore order.

The Supreme Court supported the anti-Reconstruction sentiment by issuing rulings that weakened the effects of the Fourteenth and Fifteenth Amendments. The justices ruled that the federal government had only limited power to protect Southern black voters. By July 4, 1876—the hundred-year anniversary of the signing of the Declaration of Independence—white Americans had still not decided if they really believed that "all men are created equal." By the end of that year, they had, in effect, decided—but Sojourner could not have liked their decision.

The initial results of the 1876 presidential election indicated that the victor, by a narrow margin, was Democratic candidate Samuel Tilden. However, Republicans bribed the electoral officers of Louisiana and Florida to change their voting tallies and thus switch their states' electoral votes to the Republican candidate, Rutherford Hayes. These Republicans promised that the new administration would let conservative whites regain control of the South.

With a change in the electoral vote, Hayes became the nineteenth president of the United States. One of his first acts as president was to withdraw the federal troops that were helping to protect the civil rights of Southern blacks. The action signaled that the Reconstruction era was over, and the gains that blacks had won after the Civil War would be rolled back. Despite the significance of this action, Sojourner did not have the strength to go on a speaking tour to protest against the new attempts to deprive blacks of their rights.

Rumors began to circulate that she had died or that she was too old to travel, having already celebrated her one hundredth birthday. Actually she was nearing eighty years old and living at her home in Battle Creek. Her hair had turned gray thirty years before, and now her hearing and sight had almost completely failed. The once tall and strong Sojourner Truth needed the support of a cane to walk.

In 1877, according to some accounts, Sojourner's health mysteriously improved. Perhaps her spirit was strengthened by the knowledge that wherever there was oppression, courageous people like herself were rising up to carry on the battle for freedom. In any case, her hearing returned and her eyesight sharpened dramatically. She told her friend Olive Gilbert that the Lord had "put new glasses in the window of [her] soul." A newspaper reporter who visited her at this time wrote that her gray hair had turned black again and that her skin was almost free of wrinkles. "It is the mind that makes the body," Sojourner maintained.

That next year, Sojourner went on another speaking

Sojourner TRUTH

tour, covering thirty-six different towns in Michigan. Then, at eighty-one years old, she was one of three Michigan delegates to the Woman's Rights Convention in Rochester. Later, after a grueling trip to Kansas where she spoke to newly freed slaves who were planning to homestead, Sojourner returned home for good.

Four years before Sojourner died, a Louisville, Kentucky, newspaper wrote, "The oldest truth nowadays is Sojourner." And so it seemed to the nation, because for many decades, they had heard the name of Sojourner Truth. To the general public, she seemed blessed with boundless energy, subject to rules of existence that were other than human. Despite the great age that she claimed, she never seemed to tire and would pick up new causes to champion with a vigor unknown in most people of her years. The general perception of Sojourner was wrong, however. She was very human and her health was steadily declining.

Many people were misled about Sojourner's age. They believed that she was almost a second Methuselah: One person said that she was 82 in 1868; when she met with President Grant and the senators in 1870, she was reportedly 90; close to death, she herself declared that her age was 114; her obituary put it as 108; on her gravestone, which was carved years later, her age was listed as 105. In fact, when Sojourner Truth died in 1883, she was approximately 86 years old.

Sojourner continually struggled with her health during the last twenty years of her life. Letters she dictated during those years report on the progress of her recovery from one illness or another. In the *Anti-Slavery Standard* of February 13, 1864, appeared a letter in which she wrote, "Since I have been here [Detroit] I am gaining health and strength fast. . . . I can almost walk without a cane." A few years later, a friend recorded in her diary that Sojourner's "health was quite good; she is cheerful and hopeful."

In the introduction to the 1878 edition of Sojourner's *Narrative*, Frances Titus wrote that despite various rumors of Sojourner's death, her "mind is as clear and vigorous as in middle age." She reported, however, that as far back as 1863, Sojourner had complained: "Lord, I'm too old to work—I'm too sick to hold meetings and speak to people and sell my books." What a great tribute to Sojourner's determination that despite her ill health, she was able to devote herself so tirelessly to the various causes that occupied her final years.

By the beginning of 1882, Sojourner had become gravely ill. Painful ulcers covered her arms and legs, and she became too weak to get up from her bed. She remained this way for the next year and a half. According to Olive Gilbert, "Her life's forces were spent."

Dr. John Harvey Kellogg, director of the Battle Creek Sanitarium, admitted her because she was near death. In the fall of 1883, he wrote to her friend Josephine, "In a half-reclining position on a bed, her back bolstered up with pillows. . .lay. . .Sojourner Truth. She said nothing until made aware of Mrs. Titus's presence, when she lifted her head slightly, displayed a great wrinkled and emaciated. . .face, but eyes as bright as they have ever been. Her illness. . .is very severe and causes her great pain. . .and all hope is now given up of a restoration to health."

Even in her pain and close to death, Sojourner was able to display that spirit that had become so familiar to her admirers and friends. She spoke weakly to visitors, mostly on religious subjects. She seemed completely at ease with her imminent death, feeling that God's glory was awaiting her. To a sorrowful friend who paid her a visit, Sojourner explained her peace: "I'm not going to die, honey. I'm going home like a shooting star." Sojourner was convinced through her deeply ingrained faith in God's goodness that she would return to the sky and go directly to God's bosom.

One morning early in November 1883, Gilbert visited Sojourner and found her in extreme pain. Yet when Sojourner saw her old friend, she smiled and, with a faraway look in her eyes, began to sing her favorite hymn, which she had often used to gather crowds for her speeches:

It was early in the morning,
It was early in the morning,
Just at the break of day,
When He rose, when He rose, when He rose,
And went to heaven on a cloud.

Two weeks later, at her home in Battle Creek, Sojourner Truth sank into a deep coma. She died at three o'clock on the morning of November 26, 1883. She did not fear death, she had said, for she was confident that she would be happy in heaven.

At the time of Sojourner's death, a Battle Creek newspaper reported, "This country has lost one of its most remarkable personages." A New York paper reminded its readers that "she did not seek the applause of her fellow beings, but worked quietly and with modesty."

More personal expressions of sadness about Sojourner's death came from her old colleagues Wendell Phillips and Frederick Douglass. Phillips wrote that Sojourner "was a remarkable figure in the anti-slavery movement, almost the only speaker in it who had once been a slave in a Northern state." Douglass wrote that she had been "venerable for age, distinguished for insight into human nature, remarkable for independence and courageous self-assertion."

Two days after Sojourner Truth's death, nearly a thousand people gathered at her house and formed a procession behind the black-plumed hearse that bore her body. Her coffin was decorated with the images of a cross, a sheaf of ripe grain, a sickle, and a crown. It was carried by white residents of Battle Creek to the Congregational and Presbyterian Church, and many of her fellow activists in the women's rights and abolitionist movements spoke about her "rare qualities of head and heart." At her funeral, Sojourner was remembered as a dynamic woman with strength, integrity, poise, and wit. Her friend, the Reverend Reed Stuart, delivered the funeral sermon.

A reporter described the last scene: "The long line of carriages, the hearse with its black plumes, the people— all so motionless—the cloudless sky, the great round, red sun lying low on the horizon. . ."

The sun was setting in Battle Creek's Oakhill Cemetery as Sojourner Truth was lowered into her final resting place. Crimson and gold lit up the western horizon. Gilbert later said that the sun seemed "unwilling to leave the earth in gloom." When the sun finally set, millions of stars lit up the heavens in which Sojourner had found assurance that God was watching over her. She was buried near her grandson Sammy.

In return for God's guidance, Sojourner Truth became His faithful servant, continually ignoring personal hardship in her pursuit of freedom for blacks and women. "I think of the great things of God," she said, "not the little things." Deeply devoted to turning the world "right side up," she traveled far and wide to leave an inspiring legacy to all those who face a long and difficult journey when fighting for justice and respect.

ELEVEN

During her lifetime, few tributes to Sojourner Truth's life were written. Fewer yet survived her into history. Sojourner's *Narrative* and her "Book of Life" were carefully recorded and printed by Olive Gilbert and Frances Titus. In these human documents, the reader can sense the love and respect Sojourner earned from many of her contemporaries.

The visual arts also paid tribute to Sojourner Truth. The sculptor William Wetmore Story heard Harriet Beecher Stowe's account of her meeting with Sojourner in her Andover, Massachusetts, home. He was inspired to make a statue he called the "Sibilla Libica," which was shown in the World's Exhibition in London in 1862 and attracted much critical attention.

In 1892, Frances Titus commissioned a posthumous portrait of Sojourner to be painted by the artist Frank C.

Courter from the photograph on Sojourner's *carte de visite*. This painting shows Truth seated with Lincoln, both of them looking at the Bible that the black residents of Baltimore had given the president. The painting was exhibited in the Michigan building at the 1893 World's Fair in Chicago and later hung in the Battle Creek Sanitarium until the building burned down in 1902. In 1913, an artist named Jackson, working from a photograph of Courter's work, produced another canvas of Sojourner and Lincoln, which now hangs in the Detroit Historical Museum.

Beyond these few memorials, few people carried Sojourner's memory into this century. Even in Battle Creek, where many prominent residents attended her funeral and where they held her up as the city's foremost and first famous citizen, her grave remained unmarked for thirty-three years. The only identification was the number 9 in lot 634. In 1904, the Daughters of the American Revolution launched a movement to have Sojourner Truth's grave properly marked, and in 1916, a marble headstone was finally placed on the site. When the harsh winter weather in Michigan had eroded it, the marker was replaced with a granite tombstone in 1946, which today marks Sojourner's grave.

Almost eighty years after her death, the Sojourner Truth Memorial Association of Battle Creek placed an historical marker beside her grave. This memorial association had been formed in the 1920s to raise five thousand dollars to perpetuate Sojourner's name. Dissolved during the 1930s, the group appeared later under different leadership and was responsible for providing the funds for both the historical marker and the Sojourner Truth Room in Battle Creek's Kimball House Museum.

Battle Creek is also home to Truth Drive, a road that connects streets in a housing project. Bernice Lowe, a dedicated historian who devoted over twenty years of her life to research Sojourner Truth, makes her home in Battle Creek.

Outside Battle Creek, Sojourner Truth has received little of the national attention she deserves. The Soldiers and Sailors Monument in Detroit shows the figure of a black woman crowning soldiers and sailors. Some people say that the statue represents the black people's gratitude for emancipation. Legend has it that the black woman is Sojourner, but this has not been confirmed.

In 1942, the federal government built a housing project in Detroit and named two hundred units of it the Sojourner Truth Houses. On February 28, 1942, three black families were to move into the otherwise unoccupied buildings. A mob of twelve hundred whites, armed with knives, bottles, clubs, rifles, and shotguns, prevented the families from moving into the units. Three times the police used tear gas to disperse the crowd. Dozens of people were injured, and over a hundred were arrested. Not until April of that year, with the protection of eight hundred state police troopers, were twelve black families able to occupy their apartments.

At least two libraries in other parts of the country have rooms named for Sojourner Truth.

Former New York Congresswoman Shirley Chisholm visited Sojourner's grave in April 1972 as an act of tribute from one black woman to another.

Sojourner Truth believed in peaceful dialogue and energetic persuasion. She surely would weep to see the degree of intolerance that persists more than one hundred years after her death.

When Belle became Sojourner Truth, she declared that her devotion to the truth would never die: "And the truth shall be my abiding name," she promised. Whenever people speak out against injustice and scorn oppression, they keep Sojourner Truth's ideals of justice and freedom alive.

FOR FURTHER READING

Free Indeed
by Callie Smith Grant
Features the stories of black Christians who led the stugle for equality: Dr. James W. C. Pennington, Harriet Tubman, Mary McLeod Bethune, and Rosa Parks.
ISBN 1-59310-387-5

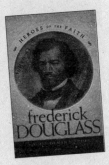

Frederick Douglass
by Rachael M. Phillips
Frederick Douglass, once a slave himself, used his God-given intelligence and melodious voice to become a powerful, articulate advocate of freedom.
ISBN 1-59310-388-3